"Of all the spiritual disciplines, prayer is often the most neglected. Yet when you look at the Scripture page after page and verse after verse exhorts us to seek the face of God through prayer! What are we missing? What has gone wrong? In this book, J.D. Greear not only provides the answers but gives us a powerful and beautiful path forward to what has become one of the most neglected but desperately needed aspects of our walks with Christ."

Dr. Matt Carter, Lead Pastor, Sagemont Church, Houston, Texas

"If you're like me, when you noticed this book on prayer, you might have thought, 'Oh no! Not prayer again!' Why is that? Why do we groan about prayer? Maybe it's because we're all too familiar with our prayerlessness, our guilt, and our failure. I get that... and the great news is that so does my friend J.D. With a pastor's heart, a firm grasp on Scripture, and a winsome, down-to-earth way of writing, he will draw you into the exciting world of joyful, bold, patient prayer. Pick up this book, read it, and then start talking to your Father who loves to hear your voice."

Elyse Fitzpatrick, Author, *Worthy: Celebrating the Value of Women*

"This book is for people like me: prayer weaklings. We've all heard about prayer warriors. Perhaps we even know a few. But it's the prayer weaklings that need help, and this book bent my wobbly knees and helped me cry out to my Father. I hope it helps you too."

Rebecca McLaughlin, Author, *Confronting Christianity*

"I met J.D. in the late 1990s, and back then he was talking about planting thousands upon thousands of churches around the world so that the gospel could be heard by everyone. And even then, at the foundation of this audacious goal was a deep dependence upon prayer. J.D. is going to teach you how to pray and why we pray, and as you learn to pray, your life will be transformed."

Dr. Derwin L. Gray, Lead Pastor, Transformation Church, Indian Land, South Carolina; Author, *God, Do You Hear Me?*

"This book is biblical, realistic, and above all hopeful. As a lifelong struggler when it comes to praying, I'm always on the lookout for books and resources that remind me of the privilege and possibility of a health~ ~~~~~ 'thout losing theologi-cal depth, game-changer you've been looki

Dav╵ 'hurch, Cardiff, Wales

D0967289

JUST

J. D. GREEAR

ASK

To my mother, Carol, who taught me to pray
by praying for me, over me, and in front of me
for as long as I can remember.

Just Ask
© J.D. Greear, 2021
Published by:
The Good Book Company

thegoodbook.com | thegoodbook.co.uk
thegoodbook.com.au | thegoodbook.co.nz | thegoodbook.co.in

Cover Design by Faceout Studio, Spencer Fuller
Design and Art Direction by André Parker

ISBN: 9781784986360 | Printed in Turkey

CONTENTS

FOREWORD

At a recent Christmas, I gave one of my teenage grandsons the bestselling book *Make Your Bed*. Written by Admiral McRaven, the former leader of the Navy Seals, this book gets down to the basics of life. Confused about your purpose in life? Make your bed! Not sure what direction to go in? Make your bed! The logic is delightful. Don't get lost in mind games—do something specific, concrete and helpful first thing in the morning. Make your bed!

J.D. Greear does the same thing with *Just Ask!* Don't get all twisted up into theological knots as to whether prayer changes things—Just Ask! Don't give into despair over something really hard and painful in your life—Just Ask! That's the wisdom of J.D.'s book. It's a simple primer of the basics of getting started with a life of prayer.

I added the exclamation mark to the title. Why? Because the "!" conveys the simplicity of asking. "Just Ask!" That's all you have to do. It's not that complicated. It also conveys the urgency. Do it today! Don't wait!

I often encourage people who are at ground zero in their prayer life to begin with just five minutes a day. Just give me five. With a couple of young men I was discipling, even five minutes proved to be daunting, so I dropped it down to one minute! And yes, once they got a taste of praying, of seeing that their Father really does hear them, that time slowly expanded. Don't overthink prayer.

Just ask.

Don't let the book's simplicity fool you. Dr. Greear does tackle and answer some of the hard questions about prayer, but he doesn't get stuck in a morass. He channels the simplicity of Jesus telling his disciples to become like little children. Little children know how to ask.

Nowhere in Scripture has the simplicity of asking struck me more than in Isaiah's great lament over the destruction of the temple in Isaiah 63 – 64. At the very center of this lament, Isaiah opens up his heart and shares why it is broken:

> From of old no one has heard or perceived by the ear,
> no eye has seen a God besides you,
> who acts for those who wait for him. (Isaiah 64:4)

That last line is the heart of a praying life. It's the simple knowledge that our Father acts for those who wait for him. There's no magic in prayer in and of itself. The "magic" is in my Father, who loves me, is for me, and acts on my behalf.

It's easy, especially as we "mature" as Christians, to miss the simplicity of just asking. Recently, my assistant, Donna, with a few deft strokes, solved an IT problem with my computer that had been bedeviling me. I was so surprised at her quickness that I asked her, "How did you do that?" She said, "I prayed." I started laughing. You wouldn't know that I'd written a book on prayer from the way I handled my IT problem. I hadn't prayed. She had. I so easily lose the childlike simplicity of "just ask."

My grandson started making his bed. You can get down on your knees at your bedside and become like a little child and just ask. It's that simple. This book will help you bend your knees and hold them in position for five minutes. If you endure, you'll be amazed at what your Father does!

Paul E. Miller, Author of *"A Praying Life"* and
"J-Curve: Dying and Rising with Jesus in Everyday Life"

INTRODUCTION

Let's be honest: most of us do not have a healthy, happy prayer life.

I'm not saying that to judge you. (I don't even know you.) I'm saying that because it's my experience, both personally and as a pastor. We struggle with prayer. The theologian D.A. Carson once said that if you really want to embarrass the average Christian, just ask them to tell you the details of their personal prayer life.

I wish he were wrong. But he's not.

"Mature" Christians often have an excellent grasp of Scripture. Many have wonderful stories of how they shared the gospel with others. More still can point to their sacrificial commitment to ministry or their faithful, consistent giving. But our prayer lives? Not so impressive.

One survey done at a major seminary found that only six percent of the students asked would set aside a time to pray each day.

Six.

And here's why our lackluster prayer lives should concern us: Jesus said, "Apart from me you can do nothing" (John 15:5). The only way to be connected to him, he said, is through abiding (15:1), and abiding implies praying. Apart from prayer, nothing happens.

"Nothing" is a pretty all-encompassing word, and Jesus chose it deliberately. Those who don't know how to pray will see little of lasting significance remain from their lives. The great 18th-century English evangelist John Wesley famously said, "I am convinced God does nothing on earth except in answer to prayer."

Jesus told his followers, "When you pray..." because he saw it as an expectation, not an optional extra for super-Christians (Luke 11:1). His half-brother James declared to a struggling church that the reason they did not have was because they did not ask (James 4:2).

If we're not asking, we're missing something big. We might, in fact, be missing everything.

JESUS' MOST IMPORTANT DISCIPLINE

You might think that if there were ever one person who didn't need to pray, it would be Jesus. I mean, when you're God the Son, shouldn't that give you sufficient self-confidence to go through the day? Yet the Gospels show us that Jesus' life was saturated with prayer. As a man, Jesus depended on communion with the Father for his strength and the fullness of the Spirit for his power. Prayer wasn't an optional add-on—some "best practice" that he wanted to model for us. It was a non-negotiable daily staple in his life: more essential to him, it seems, than eating or sleeping.

I know that's a big statement, so walk with me through Luke's Gospel for a minute and let me show this to you. Before Jesus was baptized, he prayed (Luke 3:21). As his ministry and his popularity grew, Luke records him more frequently withdrawing to pray (5:16). Before he chose his disciples, he spent the whole night in prayer (6:12). Before he presented those disciples with the ultimate question—"Who do you say that I am?"—he bathed the experience in prayer (9:18-20). After they had confessed him to be the Christ, the Son of God, he headed up a mountain with three of them to—you guessed it—pray (9:28). As he drew near to his death and experienced the agony of its anticipation, he prayed (22:39-46). In the hours before his arrest, he prayed for Peter because he knew that while he was walking towards his death for Peter, Peter would be busy denying knowing him (22:31-34). While he was nailed to the cross, he prayed for the men holding the hammers (23:33-34). And what did he do with his very last breath? He prayed: "Father, into your hands I commit my spirit!" (23:46).

When the disciples wanted to be taught by Jesus, they asked him to "teach us to *pray*" (Luke 11:1, my emphasis). Think about that. They had heard him preach great sermons. They had seen him perform great miracles. But they didn't say to him, *Lord, teach us to preach like you* or *Lord, teach us to perform miracles like you*. Instead, they said, *Lord, teach us to pray like you*. Evidently they saw that as the key—as the source of his power. If they could pray like he did, they could expect the power he had.

The point Luke is making throughout his Gospel is this: if Jesus—the divine Son of God, dwelling as a man in human flesh—felt like he could do nothing on his own and knew he needed his Father's help, strength, and guidance, why would we think we are any different? If Jesus—who had a world to save and a church to build—took time to ask his Father to give him what he needed, why would we think we are too busy to pray or too strong to need to? Why would we go through our lives with so little prayer?

Do we honestly think of ourselves as more capable than Jesus?

FOLLOWING HIS EXAMPLE

The early church were fully aware of their insufficiency for their task, which is why we see them follow the example of their Lord's devotion to prayer. Jesus had taught the apostles: "A servant is not greater than his master, nor is a messenger greater than the one who sent him" (John 13:16). Thus, the early church prayed, just as their Master had. They weren't greater than the Master. He sought the Father desperately in prayer, an example the early church imitated closely. Just as in the book of Luke the author wants to show us that Jesus depended on God in prayer, in his second volume—the book of Acts—he seeks to show us that the foundation of the early church's ministry was prayer. It was the secret behind all the explosive growth of the church in that first generation.

Let's quickly track that now through Acts. As the disciples waited for the coming of the Spirit, all the believers devoted themselves to prayer (Acts 1:14). When they chose a new apostle to replace Judas, they prayed (1:24-25). After the Spirit added 3,000 to the church on the day of Pentecost, they devoted themselves to praying—again, all of them (2:42). When they faced persecution, they responded in prayer (4:24-30). The apostles, when the church grew quickly and they realized that they were struggling with the extent of their ministry, declared they must prioritize "prayer and ...

the ministry of the word" (6:4). By the way, don't miss that the apostles saw praying as being as central to their leadership calling as preaching! In the original language, "prayer" and "ministry of the word" are written to show two equal things. Prayer, for them, was not merely a preparation for ministry; it was ministry. It was what Jesus had sent them into the world to do.

So, we see these Christians praying for the sick (9:40). They prayed for people to be released from prison (12:5). They prayed as God raised up missionaries (13:2-3). They prayed before they appointed elders (14:23).

I could go on. The point is that just as it was for Jesus, so it was for the disciples: prayer was fundamental to everything they did. Everything.

So here is my concern for our churches and our individual Christian lives today: what was fundamental for the early church has become supplemental in the 21st-century church.

Is it any wonder, then, that we are often strangers to the power that the early church enjoyed? Should it be a surprise that we lack the joy that the early Christians experienced?

We wonder why God does not do great things through us like we see in the early days of the church. But we don't ask him for those great things like they did.

We wonder why our lives don't brim with the exuberance and joy we see in Jesus and the apostles. But we don't spend time with the Father like they did.

We need, all over again, to ask Jesus to teach us to pray. That is the very simple aim of this book: that as you look at what God says about speaking to him (and hearing from him), the privilege and joy of prayer would be rekindled in you.

Here's my one driving conviction behind this book: we can enjoy the same source of power that our Lord and the early church did when we learn to depend on the Father like they did. The prophet Isaiah tells us that his arm is not shortened that it cannot save, nor his ear dull that he cannot hear (Isaiah 59:1). And he has not changed.

We just need to ask.

PART ONE

WHY WE DON'T PRAY

CHAPTER ONE

HONESTLY, DOES PRAYER REALLY DO ANY GOOD?

So you haven't put the book down yet. That's a good sign. I'll interpret that decision as you agreeing with the confession I opened the book with: we struggle with prayer.

But why?

We're not having this conversation out loud—no one can hear what is going on in your head. So, be honest...

Why do you find it so difficult to pray?

Most of us would point to some deficit in our self-discipline. We don't pray enough for the same reason we don't work out enough and don't eat enough kale salad. We just need more resolve, more determination, more self-control. Maybe we just need a more detailed plan or better resource. Maybe you were hoping for that when you picked up this book.

And maybe that's true—most of us could use a little more self-discipline. But I think there are a couple of deeper issues with our approach to praying: issues that resolutions to do better will not overcome. I think the honest reason that most of us don't pray is that we don't think it does much good.

That's right; I said it.

We all think it sometimes. I just verbalized it.

The process goes something like this. Sometimes you pray and things happen. (So far, so good.) But then sometimes you forget to pray and the thing you forgot to pray for happens anyway. (Good enough, except that it seems to undermine the whole "prayer is essential" premise.) And other times, you pray hard and nothing changes. (That one's the worst.)

So deep down we get to thinking, "I'm not sure there's any actual connection between me praying and things happening. Sometimes God answers the prayers I didn't pray, and sometimes he doesn't answer the ones I did. My prayers don't change anything. God, if he's even up there, does what he does irrespective of me."

And so we give up praying. Maybe we give up on faith altogether, whether quietly or spectacularly. (And by the way, if that's you, then I'm so glad you're reading this book—thank you for picking it up.) Most often, though, we simply become prayerless, or almost prayerless, Christians.

Believe it or not, Jesus was aware of this struggle. Remarkably, Jesus was always a safe person to bring your doubts to. We know this because, when his disciples asked him to teach them how to pray (Luke 11:1), straight after he gave them some initial instructions (which we'll come to in chapters 5 and 6), he immediately dealt with the question of whether prayer even works at all. You might think that by this point in the disciples' training, he'd have kicked out anyone who still had doubts about whether prayer worked. But Jesus heads right for this topic of discussion even with his most advanced followers.

SHAMELESS BOLDNESS

As he so often does, Jesus tells a story that we find ourselves nodding our heads along with. He imagines someone who goes to see his friend at midnight and says to him, "Friend, lend me three loaves, for a friend of mine has arrived on a journey, and I have nothing to set before him" (Luke 11:5-6). Now, that's a tough enough situation in the 21st century, but we're in first-century Judea here. There are no 24-hour grocery stores; there is no late-night take-out, no Door Dash or Uber Eats. If a guest shows up and you don't have food, they're going to bed hungry, and you're going to bed embarrassed.

But the situation gets worse. He's going over to make this request at midnight. Again, remember we're in the first century. There's no electric light, so when the sun went down, people went to sleep. Therefore, "midnight" doesn't mean here what it means for the university students at my church—an hour or two before bedtime. No, midnight means exactly what the word implies: the middle of the night. Halfway through your sleep cycle. As this guy pounds on the door, his neighbor will have been in bed for four hours already. He'll be in the midst of sound REM sleep when the noise starts up. Is it any surprise his answer is a bit short? "Do not bother me; the door is now shut, and my children are with me in bed. I cannot get up and give you anything" (v 7).

Don't miss the detail that "my children are with me in bed." In those days most people lived in one-room houses, with one large bed area for the whole family. So the loud knocking isn't just waking up dad. It's waking up everyone, including the kids. If you're a parent, I don't need to tell you how irritating this would be, because getting the family back down will likely be a several-hour ordeal. The guy outside may use the word "friend" as he calls through the door, but I'm guessing this friendship is on thin ice at this point.

Furthermore, it's not as if he has a life-threatening emergency. Yes, in the first century, hospitality mattered. You lost face if you couldn't feed a guest. But it wasn't wake-up-everyone-in-your-neighbor's-house important. No one is dying here. The guy has not come round to say, "My wife just fell down our stairs, and she's bleeding out of her ears!" No, it's "Hey, I just had some guests show up unexpectedly, and I'm out of pop tarts, and I need to borrow some from you." It's not a matter of life and death. It's just a request.

Finally, the request he is making is exorbitant. We might miss that just reading this story, but in those days loaves of bread were huge, and one loaf would feed a large family for an entire day. And he's asking for three.

So, how will the guy who is (or was) happily sleeping with his family, with plenty of bread for the next day, respond? Jesus says, "He will not get up and give him anything because he is his friend" (v 8). (In fact, after all this, they are likely not friends anyway.) He doesn't get up out of friendship. But, says Jesus, he will get up.

Why? Because of the "impudence" of the knocking man.

Some Bible versions translate "impudence" as "boldness" or "shamelessness." The man will get what he's asking for because of his impudent, bold, shameless knocking. He'll get the bread because he's one of those people who will go round to a friend's house at midnight, knock on their door, and keep knocking. The lights may be off but that won't put him off because he knows the folks inside are home, and because he knows they know he knows they're home. He's going to keep knocking till they give up trying to sleep, get up, and give him what he needs.

Jesus' point? This scene should depict your prayer time with God: "Ask, and it will be given to you; seek, and you will find; knock, and it will be opened to you" (v 10). And the implication is clear: God only gives some things in response to ongoing, patient, relentless, impudent, bold, shamelessly persistent prayer.

Or to put it another way: God delights to share his power with those who are bold enough to bother him.

Jesus' words, not mine.

PRAY, ALWAYS

I think the disciples were slow to grasp this lesson—because, seven chapters later, Luke shows us Jesus basically telling the same story again. I find it quite reassuring that the future leaders of Jesus' church, well-advanced into their ministry training, had to be taught repeatedly that prayer actually works.

And I'm pretty sure that Luke included both stories for us because he knew we'd be slow to grasp this, too. It's hard, Luke says, "always to pray and not lose heart" (18:1).

The second story teaches the same basic point but with some illuminating nuances. This time, the person doing the asking is a widow who wants "justice against [her] adversary." And the person doing the answering is a "judge who neither feared God nor respected man" (v 2-3).

So why does he give her what she wants? "Because," says the judge, "this widow keeps bothering me" (v 5).

Did you catch that? In this analogy we are the widow, and God is... That's right—in Jesus' analogy, the unjust, selfish judge represents God. If that sounds wrong to you, it should. But Jesus' purpose is not to compare God with an unjust judge but to contrast him with one. And his point is this: if even an unrighteous, selfish judge would grant answers because of persistent, relentless asking, how much more will the perfect Judge of the world—your heavenly Father, who knows how many hairs are on your head—grant answers to his children who come to ask?

In other words: perhaps the reason we don't think our prayers change anything is because we give up too soon. Maybe God doesn't seem like he's listening because he's waiting for us to bother him.

These two (rather scandalous) parables teach us three crucial points about prayer: that it should be desperate, bold, and persistent. I believe if we grasp these three truths, we will find our passion for prayer ignite anew.

PRAY DESPERATELY

One thing true of both main characters in these stories is that they are desperate. Both are entirely out of options. They would love to have had other options, but the unprepared host has nowhere else to go for food and the poor, wronged widow has nowhere else to turn for justice. She has no husband, no annuity, and no rich friends to stand up for her—the judge is her only hope.

One of the things that keeps us from praying is simply this: we fail to recognize how utterly desperately we need God's help.

If you live in the West—and particularly if you live in the United States—a "can-do" spirit is bred into you from birth. We assume that given enough time and energy, we can figure out the solution to anything. After all, it's right there in the name: I am an Ameri-can, not an Ameri-can't. (For those of you not from America, yes, we actually say that. Feel free to roll your eyes.) We are, culturally, DIY people. The largest hardware supply store in our country has the tagline "You can do it." President Obama ran for election on the slogan "Yes, we can." John F. Kennedy famously told us that the only thing keeping us from the moon was our decision not to go.

This kind of optimism and spirit of innovation can often be helpful. It's healthy to respond to a challenge by wanting to overcome it, believing you can—and working hard to do it. But this spirit is absolutely deadly when it comes to spiritual things because Jesus said, "Apart from me you can do nothing" (John 15:5). Prayerlessness comes from the fact that deep down we don't really, actually believe him when he says that. As Paul Miller, who wrote the Foreword to this book, points out in his book *A Praying Life*, if you are not praying it may well be because "you are quietly confident that time, money, and talent are all you need in life" (page 49).

Of course, we don't verbalize it in those brazen terms. It would sound weird and wrong if we actually said it out loud. But when we're honest, that's often what we believe in our hearts. We excuse our prayerlessness by saying we are too tired or too busy. And we let ourselves off the hook with that because, in our heart of hearts, we don't think we actually need to pray. Enough time, money, and talent, and you can sort things out.

Until something in your life reveals that you can't.

For me, the area of life that exploded my DIY approach was parenting. When I first became a parent 17 years ago, I read every possible book on parenting I could get my hands on. My philosophy was this: if I can become an expert at Christian parenting, then I will be able to guarantee that my kids will turn out right. (Parents, I can hear you laughing from here.)

The book that crushed this philosophy was called *Give Them Grace* by Elyse Fitzpatrick. She points out that most books on Christian parenting have the philosophy of giving you the principles and saying (usually implicitly and sometimes explicitly), if you do A, B, and C, then your kids will turn out well. I was thinking, "Exactly. That's exactly what I'm looking for, Elyse. Give me A, B, and C. Shoot, I'm ready for the next-level stuff, so if you've got D and E, lay 'em on me."

But then she points out the problem with this approach. God is a perfect Father. Yet one third of the angels he made rebelled (see Revelation 12:4). The only two humans he directly created both rebelled. And she asks whether I, the reader, think I can out-technique, out-principle, out-parent God?

She contends that the really dangerous problem with this kind of thinking—that we can DIY Christian parenting—is that it keeps us from the one thing we most desperately need, and that is to daily cast ourselves down at the feet of Jesus, looking to him for his mercy in our kids' lives to do what we cannot do.

The Bible tells us that "cursed is the man who trusts in man and makes flesh his strength" (Jeremiah 17:5). Ironically, one of the ways we can "trust in man" is by thinking that mastering biblical wisdom guarantees a healthy spiritual life. But Jesus did not save us by teaching us principles; he saved us by offering us resurrection power. Jesus did not come down to impart a manual for us to live by, but a Spirit to live in and through us. It is a tragedy to master the principles and then forget the relationship that gives them life. The apostle Paul said that this is having "a form of godliness, but denying the power thereof" (2 Timothy 3:5, KJV).

Do principles matter? Of course; learn them. But most of all, cast yourself on the mercy of God in prayer.

Our only hope—for ourselves, for our families, for our churches, for our communities—lies in God's grace. Not in our efforts or abilities. Not in our techniques or our biblical principles. You're likely nodding along to that. But do you believe that?

Because if you do, you will pray, and you will keep praying.

Your prayers will have a tone of desperation, because you know that what you most want, you cannot do. This realization has done more to drive me and my wife, Veronica, to pray together for our kids than any set of principles or disciplines. For years, we struggled to pray together consistently. Now we've got four kids, three of whom are teenagers. We pray together all the time. It's not discipline; it's desperation. I call my teenagers my "North Korean leaders"—smart enough to make nuclear bombs but not mature enough to handle them. Prayer is our only hope.

So consider your need of God. Consider it until you are desperate. That will get you praying, and praying regularly. Many of us do not need to focus on having a longer morning prayer time. One of the men whose praying I most respect once said to me he'd never prayed for longer than 20 minutes in his life. Never! But then he added that he never went longer than 20 minutes without praying. Never!

Why? Because he knew that there was never a 20-minute period in which he didn't desperately need God's help. He knocked on the door throughout the day. So can we, and so should we.

PRAY BOLDLY

The characters in Jesus' stories are not just desperate; they are bold. The hungry neighbor asked for three loaves. He didn't think, "Well if I just ask for half a loaf, then I've got more chance of getting it." No, he asked big. The widow asked for justice from a judge she didn't know, and who was known for not giving justice. But she didn't think, "Well, he doesn't even treat rich people fairly. I'm nobody; I won't bother." No, she asked big.

Remember, Jesus is not saying God is like that judge or like that friend. God's not begrudging or unjust or reluctant. Jesus is saying that God is better than them, and if even these selfish people gave what was needed, how much more will our heavenly Father? Think about it: the woman approached the judge as a stranger, but we come to God as his beloved children. She had nothing to plead in court; we have the blood of Christ. She spoke to a judge who cared little for justice and less for her; we speak to one who cares so much that he got out of the judge's chair and hung on a cross to satisfy the demands of justice on our behalf in order that he might share with us the riches of his kingdom. We never speak to a friend who is asleep but to one who never slumbers and who knows our every need: a friend who not only gives us bread from his cupboard but gives us the bread of his own torn flesh.

When we understand who we are, and from whom we are asking, we will pray boldly; we will ask big—because the closer the relationship, the bolder the asking.

You know who naturally makes requests boldly of me and I listen? My kids. If you show up at my house at 3am, let yourself into my bedroom, and wake me up to say, "I need some water," one of us is going to jail or to the hospital. To be honest, even if I opened my eyes to find my wife asking me for some water, I'd politely inquire whether she might go get it herself. But several times over the years I've opened my eyes in the middle of the night to one of my kids standing there, saying, "Dad, I need some water"—and every time I've said, "Your mom's on the other side of this bed—she'd love to help." Just kidding. Every time, I got up and helped them. My children will naturally, boldly approach me anytime they have need. They approach with undaunted confidence in my willingness and my ability to help them. And this is how God tells us to approach him. Boldly. Like children going into their dad's bedroom at any hour of the night because they need something and they know that he will help them.

In fact, right after his story about the man waking his friend to ask for bread, Jesus uses our parent-child relationships to press his point home:

> *"What father among you, if his son asks for a fish, will give him a snake instead of a fish? Or if he asks for an egg, will give him a scorpion? If you then, who are evil, know how to give good gifts to your children, how much more will the heavenly Father give the Holy Spirit to those who ask him?" (Luke 11:11-13, CSB)*

I was always confused as to why Jesus uses the word "evil" here to describe parents. Is it just a gratuitous insult? Or a free chance to press home the doctrine of total depravity?

No. It's because Jesus is trying to contrast us, at our best, with our heavenly Father to drive home the point that he is the one who we can always be sure is listening to us. Truth is, most of us are at our best with our children—they get our generosity, our thoughtfulness, our time. Even if you're stingy in every other area of your life, you're likely less stingy toward your own kids. Jesus says that if most human parents, who are still flawed and sinful—what he calls "evil"—want to meet their kids' needs, then don't you think that our perfect heavenly Father will give us what we need whenever we come to him?

WEALTHY AND GENEROUS

Many of our failures in prayer are not because we are asking for too much, but because we imagine the love of our heavenly Father as too small. Jesus tells us, in John 15, that God's purpose in our prayers is to glorify himself. How better can he do that than by putting the magnitude of his power and generosity on display through his answers?

There's a story told about Alexander the Great, who conquered for himself an empire two-thirds the size of the US while he was in his twenties (suddenly my accomplishments seem much more modest). Towards the end of his life (at 32—so at least I've got him on that one) one of his generals came to him and said, "Alexander, I have served you faithfully for years. I've never asked you for anything. Now I have one request."

"What is it?" replied the young emperor.

The general answered, "I would like you to pay for my daughter's wedding."

"Well, you have served me faithfully all these years," said Alexander. "I will happily pay for this wedding. Go and speak to my treasurer about it."

A few days later the treasurer came to talk to Alexander. "You need to punish that general," he said. "He's trying to take advantage of you. He is requesting funds for the greatest wedding the empire has ever seen. He has invited everyone. He is taking advantage of your generosity. He must be punished."

The story goes that Alexander thought for a minute and then answered.

"No. I want you to give him everything he is asking for."

The treasurer, amazed, asked Alexander why.

"Because," replied Alexander, "my general is paying me two compliments. First, he thinks I am wealthy enough to afford all this. Second, he thinks that I am actually sufficiently generous that I will do this. He is acting as though I am wealthy and generous. So I will give him his request, because in making this request, my general shows me tremendous honor."

Alexander may have ruled two million square miles of this world for a few years; but God made it all, and he rules it eternally. Look around at his creation. You have much more evidence of God's wealth than that general did of Alexander's! And look back at the cross, where God gave his Son so that his enemies could be restored to him and enjoy his fellowship forever.

So the question is: what would your requests of God—for others and for yourself—be like if you really believed that God is infinitely wealthy and infinitely generous? Here's what: they'd be bold.

PRAY PERSISTENTLY

The reason that the friend and the judge in Jesus' parables grant the requests being made of them is because they're being made persistently: because of their petitioners' "impudence" (11:8) or their "continual coming" (18:5).

Remember, this is how the early church prayed. In Acts 11, when Peter had been imprisoned, the church prayed all night for his release. All night. They did not pray for him one time in a prayer meeting and then go and read a book about how God is sovereign and glorified in all things. No, they prayed and prayed and prayed until Peter was released. Paul prayed so much for the "thorn in his flesh" to be taken away that finally God sent an angel to tell him that God had a purpose in not taking it away, and he should stop praying about it (2 Corinthians 12:7-9).

The point is not that if we ask for long enough, we can manipulate God into giving us what we ask for in exactly the form we asked for it. Sometimes, as he did with Paul, he'll say no because he has a better plan. When Jesus' friend Lazarus was sick and Lazarus's sisters, Martha and Mary, sent to Jesus and asked him to intervene and heal, Jesus did not—he allowed Lazarus to die, for he had a greater plan (John 11:1-44).

The point is that great saints pray so persistently they have to be told to stop, and that many of us miss out on God's answers because we stop a long time sooner than they did.

This is just another way that our prayer to God is supposed to mirror a child's attitude toward a good parent. We're to persist in asking. For my kids, "no" is not really an answer; it's more an invitation to extended negotiation.

In Luke 11, Jesus is not trying to unravel all the mysteries of God's sovereignty. He is telling us, *You asked me how to pray. I'm telling you how to pray. Don't give up asking until you absolutely have to.*

God answers persistent prayer.

OUR PERSISTENCE AND GOD'S GLORY

Why does God work this way? Why does he withhold his blessings until we ask for them persistently? If it's his will to give them to us, why doesn't he just give things to us the first time we ask? We'll come to this in more detail in the next chapter, but for now let me say: I can't say for sure. But I do have a guess, and here's part of it: God is glorified through our persistence. Why? Because in persisting in the request, I am showing that God is the only place I have to go.

Think about those two stories again. The guy knocking on his friend's door didn't give up. He didn't go elsewhere: *Oh, ok, well if you won't get up I have other friends and I can go bang on their doors—I'm sure one of them will come through for me when you wouldn't.* The widow didn't say, *Ok, well, I will go find another judge, then.* No, they understood that they had one hope; one person who was their only hope; and so they persisted.

When we pray persistently, we are showing that we have the same conviction about God: "God, you are the only one who can help me. I'm not going anywhere else because there is nowhere else. I'm going to stand right there because you're my only hope." Praying once or twice doesn't demonstrate that. Praying persistently does, and so it glorifies God. That is why, I think, God is delighted by, and delighted to answer, persistent prayer.

The great sixteenth-century Reformer Martin Luther had a great analogy for this. He compared it to how a parent holds something in their hand that their kid wants, and resists his attempts to get it out of his hand to test the resolve of the child. So God tests our faith by our resolve to obtain the blessing only from him.

So, if you have been praying and praying, and you don't have an answer yet, keep praying. If you have been praying and you didn't get an answer and so you gave up, get praying. Don't give up. Keep knocking. I've been a pastor for a couple decades, and if I told you all the stories I know of in just our church of faithful men and women who have prayed and prayed and prayed for things that looked impossible, and then, at the last minute, after years, something happened, something changed, an answer came—let me just say, we'd need an entire other book. These men and women had not given up. They had shown by their prayers that God is their only hope. And he responded.

This is how God so often works. One example of this that I love is as story that is told of the 19th-century evangelist and orphanage-founder George Muller (you can read more about his prayer life in Vance Christie's *Timeless Stories*). He committed to pray every day for five young men—friends of one of his sons—to be saved. He prayed daily for 18 months before the first one came to faith in Christ. (Which is a long time—have you ever prayed daily for the same thing for over 500 days without seeing an answer?) When that first friend was saved, Muller wrote in his journal that he praised God, but that there were four more left, so he would keep praying. After another five years, the second came to Christ. He kept praying. After another six more years, the third one came to Christ. He kept praying. 36 years later, Muller was an old man, and he wrote in his journal of those last two who were still unconverted, "I hope in God and I pray on and I look for the answer." It was 52 years after the third one was converted that the final two were brought to faith in Christ.

Muller had taken seriously what Jesus wanted to teach all his people: "that they ought always to pray and not lose heart" (Luke 18:1). Don't give up. Don't stop. Pray persistently.

PRAY DESPERATELY, BOLDLY, PERSISTENTLY—AND THEN WATCH

So we're back to our original question: does our prayer actually do any good? Does prayer really change things?

It does when we pray as Jesus taught us: desperately, boldly, and persistently. The 20th-century writer G.K. Chesterton once quipped that the trouble with Christianity in society was not that it had been tried and found lacking, but that it had been found difficult and left untried. I suspect the same is true of prayer. Our problem is not so much that we have prayed desperately, boldly, and persistently, and found it lacking. It is much more likely that we have lacked these things in our prayers.

But when we do pray like this, Jesus assures us that the Father responds. How could he have made it any clearer?

So, quit praying little prayers. Don't just pray that you'd get to your job on time despite the traffic; that God would help little Karen with her test; that Jesus would "just be with us." Pray big prayers, bold prayers. Don't pray out of discipline but out of desperation. And keep doing it. Because, let me tell you, when you pray that way, you have an opportunity to see God do something great in this world through you. So pray... and then watch for the answer, for Paul tells us to "continue steadfastly in prayer, being watchful in it with thanksgiving" (Colossians 4:2).

Might it be that God has responded to our prayers, but we did not have eyes to see it? As we pray in the way Jesus taught us, and watchfully expect to see prayers being answered, we overflow with gratitude that our Father has answered us. Through our prayers God teaches us that, by his grace, our prayers change the world. And that will get us praying more—and more desperately, and more boldly, and more persistently. For one of the greatest answers to prayer, you see, is God producing in you a desire to pray more.

CHAPTER TWO

BUT SERIOUSLY, WHY ISN'T GOD ANSWERING ME?

Perhaps you read the last chapter, and you are still having trouble with the feeling that God isn't listening to you. Because you have prayed desperately, persistently, and boldly. You have not given up. But still, silence.

I want you to know that I have been in this place many, many times. If it helps, some of the greatest Christians in history have too! The great British scholar C.S. Lewis, in his book *A Grief Observed*, which he wrote after the untimely loss of his wife to bone cancer, lamented how God seemed so close to him in moments of happiness and gratitude, but...

> *"Go to Him when your need is desperate, when all other help is vain, and what do you find? A door slammed in your face, and a sound of bolting and double bolting on the inside. After that, silence. You may as well turn away. The longer you wait, the more emphatic the silence will become. There are no lights in the windows.*

It might be an empty house. Was it ever inhabited?
It seemed so once. And that seeming was as strong
as this. What can this mean? Why is He so present
a commander in our time of prosperity and so very
absent a help in time of trouble?" (page 18)

(Somehow this never seems to make anyone's "Favorite C.S. Lewis Quotes" on their Pinterest page.)

Have you been there? I have.

I want to suggest five biblical reasons why God may choose not to answer a prayer in the way we wish he would. I'm not saying that all of these things are going on in your life or your heart every time you don't experience the answer to prayer that you seek. (In fact, it would be impossible for them all to be happening.) I'm simply offering a handful of possible reasons to consider.

"Unanswered" prayer always stings, but when we consider what God might be up to in his supposed silence, it can lessen some of that sting. Corrie ten Boom, who survived a Nazi concentration camp, said that any suffering becomes bearable when you know its purpose!

REASON 1: YOU MAY NOT BE HIS CHILD

First things first. It's worth asking yourself: am I a Christian? I know that's a stark question just to put out there, but it's a necessary one. A lot of people throw up a "Hail Mary" prayer, don't seem to get an answer, and then give up on God. The problem is that they are not praying as God's children. To them, God is like a cosmic force in the sky whose power you can tap into as a last resort. Prayers are like the rubs on the proverbial magic lamp to get a divine genie to grant them a wish. They've never surrendered themselves to God, giving themselves fully to him.

God's promises always to answer prayer are extended only to his children (John 9:31). Nowhere in Scripture does God ever promise to answer the prayer of someone outside of his family—that is, someone who has not turned from their sin and surrendered to Christ, receiving his offer to forgive their sins based on his finished work at the cross.

That's not to say that God never answers prayers of non-Christians, however. Sometimes he does, because he is compassionate and gracious, and he is free to do what he wants. Scripture gives us numerous accounts of God answering the prayers of unbelievers. It's simply to say he hasn't promised to do so. Just as I am obligated to my kids in a special way, so God obligates himself to his.

This may strike you as exclusive—even mean. But in fact it is the opposite—because God wants everyone to become his child by putting their faith in Jesus his Son. Jesus said:

> "But as many as received Him, to them He gave the right to become children of God, to those who believe in His name." (John 1:12, NKJV)

He wants to include everyone in his family—as many as will receive his offer, whatever their background, their past, their flaws or personal shortcomings. His offer could not be more inclusive. Anyone—anyone—can become his child by accepting him as Lord and receiving him as Savior. If you do so, he will begin to hear and answer your prayers the way he does for each and every one of his other children.

I don't want to assume you're a Christian just because you picked up a book on prayer. And I don't want you to assume that, either. Going to church, following a moral code, being a good parent or ethical worker—none of these things make someone a child of God. Belief in God doesn't make you a Christian. Only receiving God's offer to become his child, through faith in the finished work of his Son, does. So, before you consider anything else, make sure you have this question settled. Is God merely your Creator, your Judge, and a potential help in time of trouble? Or, through Jesus, has he become your Lord, your Savior, and your Father?

REASON 2: GOD MIGHT BE CHANGING YOU

Second, God may not be answering you right now in the way you want because something in you needs to change. The Scriptures are clear that sometimes God does not answer because we do not approach him with the right posture, perspective, or purposes.

James, the author of the New Testament letter that bears his name (and who happened to be Jesus' half-brother) is really clear about this. He tells a group of believers, who are wondering why their lives are not filled with more blessing, that first "you do not have, because you do not ask" (4:2).

But sometimes you ask, he continues, and still do not receive...

> "... because you ask wrongly, to spend it on your passions." (v 3)

"Passions" in the original Greek language is a word with connotations of adultery. James is saying, "Sometimes

God doesn't answer your prayers because you pray like an adulterer." That is a stark image. How might we pray like an adulterer?

Imagine a man approaches his wife and says, "When we married, you pledged to fulfill my romantic needs." She cautiously nods her head as he continues: "What I have determined I need romantically is your friend Katy. Can you arrange a date with her for me?"

This man is not going to receive a positive answer to his request. When they were married, his wife did not pledge to be his liaison for romantic encounters; she pledged to be those things in herself.

We pray like adulterers when we ask God for something to fulfill a need in us that we should be finding in God. When I need the job, the health, the marriage partner, the restored relationship so that I can have joy, God says, *Why are you not finding your joy in me?*

I know some parents who prayed for years for a wayward son, and God didn't bring him back. And a decade after they started to pray, they realized that it wasn't only their son who was wayward; it was them, too. They had spiritual issues that they needed to deal with. There were things about them that they needed God to change. Had God answered their prayer the first time they asked it, or even just the hundredth time they asked it, they would not have seen their need to change and would not have had the humility to ask God to make those changes.

So, unanswered prayer is often God's way of purifying us. It forces us to ask why we want the answer, and what the passion of our request shows us about where we find security, joy, and significance. While God loves to fill our lives with tangible expressions of his goodness, he wants us to find those things primarily in him.

God's highest purpose in our lives is not giving us "stuff," but making us into the image of Christ: "And we know that for those who love God all things work together for good" (Romans 8:28). That is one of the most famous verses in Scripture because it sounds so reassuring, but there's a challenge in it when we read on and understand what God says is "good": "those whom he foreknew he also predestined to be *conformed to the image of his Son*" (v 29, my emphasis). The highest good that God is working for in your life is to make you like Jesus. Our ultimate happiness is based on our conformity to Christ. God may withhold an answer today because he knows it will lead you to be less Christ-like tomorrow. If answering our prayers in a decade means we will grow more Christ-like each day till then— as we see ways in which our passions and priorities are more like this world's than Christ's—then we shouldn't be surprised when God delays his response.

And when we look at it this way, we can praise him for those delays, even as we persist in our requests.

REASON 3: GOD HAS A GREATER PLAN

Third, God might not answer your prayers the way that you want because your prayers don't align with the good things God is pursuing in you and in the world. It's easy to acknowledge but hard to embrace: God's plans are always better.

That's hard to swallow because sometimes what we're asking God for feels so right, and, based on our perspective, seems like it would be right in line with God's will.

I'm not talking about asking God for something you know is not God's will, like God helping you cook the books at work or hide an illicit affair from your spouse. Of course God won't help you there. Rather, I'm talking about prayers that feel righteous. Prayers that feel like you're asking God to do something he'd want to do. Help for someone who is hurting. Financial relief. Restoring a relationship. Saving someone.

Keep in mind that God's wisdom is as high above ours as his power is above ours. (He would not be much of a God if that weren't the case.) He spoke the septillion stars of the universe into existence with a word; I can't lift my mattress over my head. If his wisdom exceeds mine to that same degree, then it makes sense that much of what he sees as best will not immediately make sense to me.

As a dad, I turned down a number of my toddlers' requests, not because I didn't love them but because I did. My 4-year-old didn't understand how having his own personal iPad available to him 24/7 in his room could possibly be damaging to him. But I did, so I said no. Or why putting the fork in the wall socket is not a good idea when it looks as if it was designed for that. But I did, so I said no.

Any parent understands that. So, which then do you think is greater—the gap between my 4-year-old's understanding of what is "best" and mine, or between our understanding and God's?

Because that gap exists, we can expect that God will sometimes not answer our prayer the way that we want. I love this line from Tim Keller's book *Prayer*:

> *"God will either give us what we ask or give us what we would have asked if we knew everything he knows."*
>
> (page 238)

Sometimes you just have to trust him. God has made known to us the endpoint of his plan for this world—his people will enjoy him forever as all things are brought into submission to and the joy of Christ (Ephesians 1:3-12). He has not made known to us most of the details for how he will get us there. We just have to trust him. As Paul memorably puts it:

> *"Oh, the depth of the riches and wisdom and knowledge of God! How unsearchable are his judgments and how inscrutable his ways!*
>
> *"'For who has known the mind of the Lord, or who has been his counselor?'" (Romans 11:33-34)*

There is no one, including you and me, who can put our hand up and answer that question: "Ooh, me! I know his plans! I gave him some advice he needed on how this thing should play out!" No—all we know is that we don't know. And so sometimes we will pray things that heaven is pleased to hear but that aren't heaven's wishes. I love how John Piper explains it:

> *"At any given point, God is pursuing about 10,000 different good things in your life, and you are usually aware of only about three of them." (desiringgod.org/articles/god-is-always-doing-10000-things-in-your-life, accessed March 19, 2021)*

Ironically, this awareness of what we're not aware of gives us confidence as we pray, because we know that God is not going to overturn his sovereign, untraceable, and glorious plan just because we're too short-sighted to understand it. In fact, the apostle John makes just this connection, linking confidence in prayer with knowing that God may not answer our prayer:

"This is the confidence that we have toward [God], that if we ask anything according to his will he hears us. And if we know that he hears us in whatever we ask, we know that we have the requests that we have asked of him." (1 John 5:14-15, my emphasis)

When we pray, we come to a Father who will sometimes say no to a good request, just as earthly fathers sometimes do—not despite their love for their child but *because* of it.

I have a friend who told me he would have been married to several different women if God had said yes to every one of his requests for romantic fulfillment. (In the immortal words of that great theologian Garth Brooks, sometimes we should thank God for unanswered prayer.) So we ought to say as we pray, "God, I think this is your will, but if it's not, then I trust you as a good Father to give me what I ought to have and what furthers your plan. Not my will, but yours be done."

My guess is that, if you think about it, you can already can look back over your life and see places where you passionately prayed for something and couldn't, at the time, understand why God wouldn't give it to you. But now you realize that if God had given you what you asked for, it would have been disastrous for you. That raises the question: if already, with only limited time and perspective, you can see a good reason for some of God's unanswered prayers, don't you think, given enough time and perspective, you'll one day see a reason for all of them? So even as we keep asking God persistently for those things we ache for and that appear to us to be in line with his will, we do so with an understanding that if he chooses to say no, one day we will see why he answered that way—and agree with him.

REASON 4: GOD DOES NOT OFTEN REWRITE THE RULES

Fourth, prayer is not given to us as a tool to lazily rewrite the natural order God has set up. Miracles are, by definition, rare. God does not typically rewrite the laws of nature through prayer. Sicknesses, typhoons, rainstorms, viruses—these things are in our world because this world is fallen. And while it is God's will to eradicate this brokenness, God does not routinely interrupt the way the world runs to do so. Does he sometimes perform miracles in these realms? Yes, which is why it is right to pray for them. Does he tell us to abandon natural processes and just pray? No.

This is why the outcome of sports matches are not usually determined by which team has the best prayer discipline. If you're a coach, your time is better spent working on your tactics than asking God for a miracle. It is rare that God gives an out-of-shape, poorly practiced player the ability to overcome a superior one just because Aunt Margaret was on her knees at game time. The reason you got a bad grade on that test was probably because you didn't study well for it, not because you cut your prayer time by five minutes. Your company lost the sell because another company worked harder to perfect the product and pursue the relationships.

In the same way, it is not right for us to pray that God would "magically" save everybody in Afghanistan tonight—that he would appear to everyone in a dream and give them faith in Jesus, and stop there. Though that prayer aligns with part of what we know God wants (1 Timothy 2:3-4; 2 Peter 3:9), it also attempts to circumvent the process that God has set up for how people come to salvation. God uses his church to preach the gospel to reach the nations (Acts 1:8). Thus, our prayer should focus on God raising up missionaries, not just raining down miracles. Our prayers should conform to the pattern of God's plans as much as possible.

Of course God can knock a man off his horse while he is on the road to Damascus to kill Christians. And praise him that he did so. But is this the kind of mission strategy God intends to make his main means of winning the nations? No. He has made his plan known: he calls his people into the hard, costly, privileged work of mission. That involves prayer, but it does not only involve prayer; it also involves giving and going. So, we should pray that God would raise up missionaries for Afghanistan. We should pray that God would show us if we ourselves are those he is raising up to go to Afghanistan. We should pray that, if we are not to be given that great calling, God would show us how we can give sacrificially for the mission. We should pray that God would anoint the words of those missionaries with unusual power and that he would give Muslims in Afghanistan ears to hear the message as it is preached to them. But merely praying that God would intervene directly to save every soul in Afghanistan is ignorantly naïve at best and lazily disobedient at worst.

Here is one more angle on this. Quite often we ask God to deliver us from the very means that God has told us he uses to grow us. Paul told the believers at Antioch that it was "through many tribulations [that] we must enter the kingdom of God" (Acts 14:22). Suffering, Paul explains repeatedly in his letters, is how God prepares us for his kingdom. Peter tells us that "to this you have been called"—that God uses trials like a furnace to purify our faith so that it comes out beautiful like gold (1 Peter 2:21; 1:7). Many of us say we want great faith, but we demand that God remove us from any situation where we'd actually have to show any! What we regard as an inconvenient diversion he intends as divine direction. God is after much bigger things in your life than granting you a path of ease; he wants you to treasure and trust him.

That doesn't mean we should pursue suffering like we are gluttons for punishment or as if suffering is some sacred status that super-spiritual Christians are supposed to enjoy. When we experience pain, it is natural and right to ask God to deliver us from it. After all, Paul did: "Three times I pleaded with the Lord about [a thorn given me in the flesh], that it should leave me" (2 Corinthians 12:8). Paul was not sitting around asking God to make it hurt more. We should, with Paul, ask for deliverance. But we can expect that God will sometimes answer us in the same way he answered Paul: *No, this suffering will remind you and show others that my grace is sufficient, and that my strength is enough for you.*

Sometimes, God is more interested in producing his strength in you is than taking your suffering from you.

John Newton, the 18th-century slave trader turned pastor and hymn writer, wrote a series of letters as an old man. In one of them he spoke of how he had been praying to be delivered from an inward weakness for 60 years—and here he was, in his late 80s, and it was still as bad as ever. For years, he confessed to a pastor friend in this letter, he could not understand why God would not answer this prayer, since he was simply asking for freedom from a temptation and that had to be God's will! But now, as an octogenarian, he realized that God had used the ongoing presence of this struggle to remind him how desperately he needed his grace, and his awareness of that need for grace made him a better help to people who needed grace. This side of heaven, the best evidence of growth in grace is a growing awareness of how desperately we depend on grace, not getting ourselves to a place where we feel like we no longer need it.

Maybe God is leaving you with a struggle that you have been desperately praying he would take away because he wants you to learn to cling to his grace. Maybe you struggle with same-sex attraction. Or with dissatisfaction over singleness. Or with greed. Or with anger. And God has not taken it from you, despite your prayers. Could it be because he wants you to learn to fight for holiness? Could it be because he wants you to be a testimony to your friends that God is better than the desires of your heart? Could it be because he wants you to understand him more fully and know him more intimately through wrestling with this issue? Could it be because he wants to save you from pride and increase your humility? Could it be because he wants you to stand in glory one day fully aware of how little you deserve to be there—a testimony to his grace, not your willpower? Not there because you conquered sin in your life, but because he did at the cross?

The church already has enough proud, self-righteous Pharisees. Maybe he leaves you with that struggle so that you will magnify his grace.

REASON 5: MAYBE GOD IS SAYING "WAIT"

We often think there are only two possible answers to our prayers: yes or no. But there's a third option: not yet. All the promises of God are yes in Christ Jesus, but some of them we have to wait for. We have to wait for some for many days; others for many years; some until the final resurrection itself.

Revelation 5 – 10 is a beautiful, if at times unsettling, picture of Jesus in heaven, about to bring the final days and his judgment and re-creation. In this vision, the apostle John sees bowls of incense around the throne, and John says these bowls represent the prayers of God's people. An angel begins to pour them out (Revelation 8:3-5). And it seems this is a picture of vast quantities of prayers prayed by the church through the ages finding their fulfillment.

Maybe you are praying for the restoration of a relationship, or wholeness for a broken mind or body, or an end to loneliness, or for justice; and God is saying, *I'm not going to give you that in this chapter of your life, here on earth. But I will answer it one day, when my Son returns and makes all the sad things untrue and makes all things new.* Metaphorically speaking, God keeps those prayers in a bowl, ready to answer in ways beyond any we can ask or even imagine, for eternity. All the promises of God are yes in Christ Jesus. Every promise God makes will be yours. It may not, despite your prayers, be yours in this little vale of tears that we call life in this world—but it will be yours for eternity. In a sense, every prayer that is answered in this life is a tiny foretaste of what life will be like in the recreated heavens and earth with our Lord.

WHAT UNANSWERED PRAYERS DO NOT MEAN

Sometimes, however, no matter how many times you analyze your unanswered prayer through our five-part grid, you still can't understand why God is not doing what you asked. And I can't tell you what that means or what you may be missing. But I can confidently tell you what it doesn't mean. If you are a child of God, a seemingly unanswered prayer does not mean that you have been forsaken.

Here's how I know that. The greatest "unanswered" prayer in history was uttered in a place called the Garden of Gethsemane, by one referred to by God as "my beloved Son in whom I am well pleased."

On the night before he died, Jesus prayed, three times:

"Father, if you are willing, remove this cup from me."
(Luke 22:42)

All three times Jesus was met with complete and utter silence. An angel came to strengthen him (v 43), but the agony was not removed and the plan was not changed (v 44, 47-48). The Father had always radiated with openness and intimacy whenever his Son called upon him, and here, in the moment when his beloved Son needed him the most, the Father turned his face away.

Why? God was doing that with Jesus so he would never have to do it with us. In the crucifixion, the Father "made him who knew no sin [Jesus] to be sin for us, that we might become the righteousness of God in him" (2 Corinthians 5:21, CSB).

This means that of all the things I might wonder with regard to an unanswered prayer, I never have to wonder what it means about how God feels about me. The cross shows me that any reason that would ever make God turn away from me was laid on Jesus, and the Father turned away from him as he hung there in my place.

God placed my sin on Jesus so that he would never turn away from me. I can be sure that "he who did not spare his own Son but gave him up for us all" will "also with him graciously give [me] all things" (Romans 8:32). And I can be confident that if Jesus did not abandon me in his darkest hour, when the judgment of his Father was literally squeezing the life out of him, he has not turned his back on me in my dark hours, even when I feel like he's not listening.

I can't give you the final explanation for what your unanswered prayer means. But I can tell you, if you are God's child, that it cannot mean that God has forsaken you. The cross assures you that he's always listening, that he'll never turn away, and that not even death itself can thwart his good purposes for you. That's a truth you can build a life on: a truth that can anchor you in any storm.

YOU CAN TRUST HIM

All that is to say, we can trust God with the prayers that he has not answered in a way we can see or in the way we would like. As we saw in the last chapter, Jesus pointed out that no loving father, "if his son asks for a fish, will instead of a fish give him a serpent; or if he asks for an egg, will give him a scorpion" (Luke 11:11-12). Neither will God.

And you can turn that around. Just as no good parent will give a scorpion to a kid who asks for a fish, no good parent will give a scorpion to a kid asking for a scorpion thinking it was a fish. Sometimes what seems like "fish" to us is actually a scorpion. I don't give my kids everything they ask for, no matter how much they want something. I want what is best for them, and that is not always the same as what they think is best. God is the same.

Again, sometimes God answers our prayers by giving us what we would have asked for if we knew what he knew. Sometimes he says, *I know you're asking for this, but that's not a fish—that's a scorpion! But you can't see it, so I'm going to give you something else.* He may not always give us what we ask for, but if we are his children, he will give us what we need.

I don't know why God did or did not answer a particular prayer. I don't know why he did not answer your prayer when your mom lay dying, or when you were being abused, or when you wanted kids but just couldn't get pregnant, or...

What I do know, though, is that you have a heavenly Father whom you can trust: that "no good thing does he withhold from those who walk uprightly," so that "blessed is the one who trusts in you" (Psalm 84:11-12). The reason I know that, and the reason that you can know that, is the cross. God is your Father, and you are his precious child. So you can leave your request at his feet and can trust that whatever he's doing—even when he's not doing what you think he should be doing—it is for your good.

To be honest, I have a hard time doing this. When I pray about something that is bothering me, I try to lay it at the feet of Jesus and trust him with it. And then I get off my knees, and I tend to pick it up again and put it back on my shoulders, as though I can bear the burden better than the one who bore the cross. But the cross tells me that I can leave it with him, and that I must.

There is sweetness and peace in being able to lay our greatest desires and needs at his feet, knowing that he has never failed any of his children in history. He will not fail you.

What a friend we have in Jesus,
All our sins and griefs to bear,
And what a privilege to carry
Everything to God in prayer.

Even when we have to wait for the answer.

CHAPTER THREE

DO MY PRAYERS CHANGE GOD'S MIND?

Life contains many realities that blow your mind. For instance, the guy who voiced Miss Piggy in the Muppets was also the voice of Yoda in *Star Wars*. I know, I know... go ahead and Google it.

Told you.

Here's another one: there are no kids left on earth who were born in the 20th century.

And then there are the big questions, such as, when I'm in a restaurant, why do I call the guy bringing my food the "waiter" when I'm the one who's waiting? Or, why do the hairs on your eyebrows stop once they get to be an inch long, but the hairs on your head don't show that same restraint? Or, did the person who decided to call a bed a bed realize that the word "bed" is shaped... like a bed?

Life is full of meaningless little mysteries, but sooner or later, as we think about praying, a significant one pops in our head: do our prayers actually alter God's plans? Does what you and I say to God convince God to do something that he was not otherwise planning to do?

The simple answer is no: you don't command God, nor do you offer reasoning to him that he hadn't thought of and which makes him revise his plans.

Has it ever dawned on you that nothing has ever dawned on God? God never responds to our prayers by saying, *Oh yeah, I forgot about that,* or *You're right; that's a good point that I hadn't thought of.* God's purposes are eternal, and his wisdom is inscrutable. He knows the end from the beginning and everything—*everything*—works out in conformity with the foreordained purposes of his will (Ephesians 1:11, NIV). He is never surprised, never taken aback, and never thwarted. Never.

But that "simple" answer leads to a difficult question—one that subconsciously saps our motivation to pray. If God is going to do what he's going to do anyway, regardless of whether I pray or not, what's the point of praying? Why make the effort to get up early or turn off the TV to speak to him, when it makes no difference because everything's already pretty much mapped out?

Great question. Let me begin to answer by going back in history a few thousand years.

GOD CHANGES HIS MIND. SORT OF.

In Exodus 32, God's people have been rescued from slavery in Egypt and, under Moses' leadership, they are on their way to the promised land. Under God's command, they've stopped to worship at Mount Sinai (Exodus 3:12; 19:1-6), and Moses is up the mountain, receiving the Ten Commandments, the rest of the law, and the designs for the tabernacle-tent where God will dwell among his people.

But Moses is gone longer than the people expected, so they jump to a ridiculous conclusion: Moses and God have now abandoned them (32:1). It makes no sense, given that God has just delivered them from the most powerful empire of their day through ten supernatural plagues and then by splitting apart a sea, followed by sustaining them on their journey with miraculous bread and meat falling from the sky each day. But the Israelites jettison reasonable thought in a moment of panic. They decide that the God who delivered them from Egypt and has met their daily needs is not sufficient—that they need a new, more capable God. And so they take off all their jewelry—the very stuff that God had caused the Egyptians to give them on their way out of Egypt—to mold a new "god" for themselves: a golden calf which they can carry around for protection. Their worship of this new god descends into an all-night orgy. It's a disaster.

Meanwhile, back at the top of the mountain, God says to Moses, "Go down, for your people, whom you brought up out of the land of Egypt, have corrupted themselves … I have seen this people, and behold, it is a stiff-necked people. Now therefore let me alone, that my wrath may burn hot against them and I may consume them, in order that I may make a great nation of you [Moses]" (v 7, 9-10).

Sounds like a pretty firm plan from God: *My mind is made up. Move out of my way.*

How does Moses respond? He reasons with God to change his mind.

> "*Moses implored the LORD his God and said, 'O LORD, why does your wrath burn hot against your people, whom you have brought out of the land of Egypt with*

> *great power and with a mighty hand? ... Turn from*
> *your burning and anger and relent from this disaster*
> *against your people. Remember Abraham, Isaac, and*
> *Israel, your servants, to whom you swore by your own*
> *self, and said to them, "I will multiply your offspring*
> *as the stars of heaven, and all this land that I have*
> *promised I will give to your offspring, and they shall*
> *inherit it forever."" (v 11-13)*

This is downright brash, right? *God,* Moses prays, *these are not MY people; they are YOURS. Have you forgotten what you said you would do for Abraham's family? Well, this is Abraham's family, in case you forgot. Your name is on the line, because this was your promise, not mine. I just don't see how you can do this, God.*

And then follows, in my opinion, the four most jarring words in the book of Exodus:

"And the LORD relented." (v 14)

Literally, the word "relented" is "repented": "changed his mind." Before you rush to theology, just read it at face value. Don't explain it away. The writer of Exodus (Moses) would have us believe that God was intending to do one thing in verse 7 until Moses persuaded him to do the opposite in verses 11–13.

Wait, what?

What makes this even more confusing is that Moses wrote elsewhere that "God is not man, that he should lie, or a son of man, that he should change his mind" (Numbers 23:19). "Change his mind" in the Hebrew there is the same word that is translated "relented" in Exodus 32:14, and Moses wrote both books. In other words, in one place, Moses says that God changed his mind; and in another, he tells us that God never changes his mind.

What is going on?

THREE TRUTHS TO HOLD IN TENSION

When my friend, the pastor and author David Platt, preached on Exodus 32 at the Together for the Gospel conference in 2014, he said that in the picture of God presented here there are three truths we must reckon with. These are truths we have to hold in tension because on the surface they look like contradictions. But truths like these in the Bible are not so much contradictions to be resolved as they are tensions to be managed.

If you're the accountant type or an ISTJ or an Enneagram 1, non-resolution tension-management likely annoys you, so let me remind you of a very important "rule of engagement" when it comes to thinking about God: God is bigger than us, and our minds are far too small to match his, so we need to get used to not being able to resolve everything. Many scientific mysteries—seeming contradictions—are resolved by an increase in knowledge. It looked as if nature contained an irreconcilable contradiction, but that was because there was some aspect of reality we hadn't discovered yet. If it's that way with nature, how much more so with God?

There are going to be truths that we cannot get our heads round. Instead of concluding that they therefore must be contradictions (making our limited and faulty intellects the arbiter of what is possible), or truths that we must choose between, we should hold them in tension—even if they push our cognitive limits to the brink of collapse.

Truth number one: *God's purposes are unchanging.*

That's what Numbers 23:19 tells us in no uncertain terms. God is not a man. He never learns anything new. He doesn't gain some insight or go through some experience that makes him re-evaluate his plans. He doesn't change his mind. As he says to his prophet Isaiah:

> "I am God, and there is no other;
> I am God, and no one is like me.
> I declare the end from the beginning,
> and from long ago what is not yet done,
> saying: my plan will take place,
> and I will do all my will.
> I call a bird of prey from the east,
> a man for my purpose from a far country.
> Yes, I have spoken; so I will also bring it about.
> I have planned it; I will also do it." (Isaiah 46:9-11, CSB)

And Paul says the same thing. We've already seen this in Ephesians 1 and Romans 11. Here's another place where he sums it up: in Colossians 1:17 he says of Christ Jesus, "He is before all things, and in him all things hold together." In other words, nothing happens outside of his plan or beyond his control.

Truth number two: *God's plans are unfolding.*

In Exodus 32, God changes his course of action based on Moses' prayer. Notice, by the way, that it's God who actually creates the moment of crisis, setting up circumstances to give Moses a chance to argue with him. It's God who tells Moses what is going on at the foot of the mountain—Moses had no idea until then! It's God who has made the promise that Moses quotes back at him. In other words, God placed Moses into a situation in which Moses would see the problem, remember the promise, and then petition God to change the course of action he'd announced.

God wanted Moses to ask this, so he sovereignly put Moses in a place where he would see the problem and then remind God of his promise, which God would then agree to uphold. God's true intentions weren't revealed all at once. He unfolded them to Moses over time.

Truth number three: *our prayers are instrumental.*

Moses' prayer, when we look at it in real time, really did change things. We have to take the text at face value. Without Moses' prayer, God would have destroyed Israel. Of course, we see that God set things up for Moses to pray that prayer, but, nevertheless, Moses' words were instrumental in getting God to change his course of action.

So what if Moses had not bothered to pray? Would that have meant that God wouldn't have saved them—that that wasn't God's will after all? Does that mean that if God wants us to pray for someone and we don't, then they won't be saved even though it is God's will? Or would he just get someone else to pray for them instead? This makes your head spin (just as it did when you first found out that Miss Piggy and Yoda are voiced by the same person, but a thousand times faster).

But this story is not in the Bible to trip us up in a net of philosophical speculation. For help, let's turn to the 19th-century Princeton theologian A.A. Hodge:

> *"Does God know the day that you'll die? What do you think? Yes. Has he appointed that day? Yes he has. Can*

you do anything to change that day? No. Then why do
you eat? To live! What happens if you don't eat? You
die. Then if you don't eat and die, would that be the
day God had appointed for you to die?"
(Evangelical Theology, pages 92-93)

Good question, right? Sounds like the same trouble we have with Moses' story. And Hodge's point (and I'm paraphrasing here) is this: *Quit asking stupid questions and just eat. Eating is the preordained way that God has appointed for living.*

In just the same way, prayer is a preordained way that God has appointed for executing his will on earth. Just as we eat today because it keeps us alive, even while we simultaneously know we cannot change the appointed date of our death, so we pray because it is the means by which God does his work on earth. Just as God has hardwired our bodies to run on food, so he has hardwired his purposes so that they are actualized by prayer.

So this story is not an invitation to become mired in mysteries about the decrees of God. It's a summons to consider how God has put you into a place to intervene. It's an invitation to pray.

On that day and on that mountain, Moses did not dwell on the unchangeable purposes of God. He focused instead on the unchanging promises of God and applied them to his situation. And so he prayed, and in the unfolding story of God's unchanging purposes, God used his prayers to save a nation—a nation that would have been doomed without them.

Did God have mercy on the Israelites because that was part of his immovable plan for his people? Yes. Did God have mercy on the Israelites because Moses bravely, boldly implored God not to destroy them? Also yes.

Put together those three truths—the unchanging nature of God's plans, the unfolding revelation of those plans, and the instrumentality of our prayers in bringing about those plans—and what do we have?

God sovereignly places people in certain situations precisely for the purpose of them praying his promises.

And that's why he has put you where you are. Think about your own circumstances. Look at all the problems you see around you and perhaps within you: the broken relationships, the people far from grace, the dysfunctional situations. God put you there—right there. He put you there to see the problems, to remember his promises, and to pray for him to work powerfully. Wherever you are—whatever your family and whatever your neighborhood—you are not there by accident but by divine appointment. You are his emissary there. Do your prayers change things? You better believe it.

By his divine power God sovereignly puts you in a situation to see a problem and change it through your prayers.

WHAT WE DO IN LIFE ECHOES IN ETERNITY

This truth—that the system is, in effect, rigged—should spur us to action. The way to know we've misunderstood the meaning of God's sovereignty is if it keeps us from doing things. Truly understanding God's sovereignty means that we understand that God has sovereignly put us in a particular place as an instrument of his blessing. His work on earth flows through channels, and those channels are our faith-filled prayers and faith-filled obedience.

Once I was flying to Taipei to visit some missionaries, and on the cross-ocean leg of the flight I sat next to a woman whom I noticed was reading a book by David Jeremiah, the hugely popular radio preacher and a personal mentor of mine. So I struck up a conversation with her.

"Where are you headed?" I asked. (Yes, I literally said that. Not until I said the words did it strike me how silly they were. We were all going to the same place: Taipei).

"What are you going to be doing there?" I followed up. This proved to be a better question. She told me she'd retired a couple years before.

"I made a lot of money really fast, but I'm kind of restless, and I really need to find myself," she said. "I'm just still not settled in life. I am on a search for the divine. I'm looking for God."

"Does he live in Taipei?" I asked.

"No," she laughed. "As far as I know, God doesn't live in Taipei. I'll be honest with you. I've had a really disappointing experience so far. This is my second trip there. I'm really attracted to the way of life over there, but I'm really not any closer to answers than when I started.

"I was there for several months, and came back to the United States because my sister has gotten really sick and we don't think she's going to make it that much longer. And I know that she might pass away, and because we're about the same age, I might pass away... I'm just so confused and I'm not really sure. I'm not really sure of anything right now."

I asked, "Well, what's with the David Jeremiah book?"

"Well," she said, "I heard him on the radio, and he sounded like he knew God. So I thought, 'I'll buy his book, and maybe he can lead me to God.'"

"What have you thought as you read it?" I asked.

"I don't know," she replied. "I have only read a few pages, and I'm confused, and I don't know where to turn. Just yesterday, I prayed, 'God, if you're out there or if you're up there, would you please reveal yourself to me?'"

"Ma'am," I said, "I don't want to be too presumptuous, but I think God might have answered your prayers. We've got eight hours. Let's go."

I pulled out my Bible and walked her through the life of Jesus. She read passage after passage out loud. You could see the light coming on with the turn of every page. After about two hours, I asked her, "How many people do you think are on this plane?"

"About 250."

"And out of all those people," I said, "you and I got assigned to sit next to each other. You have prayed for God to show himself to you. Is this a coincidence? I'm not anything special, but I'm God's instrument in this moment, and I can tell you with the authority of his word that he wants you to belong to him."

It was then, somewhere over the Pacific, that she bowed her head and accepted Christ's offer to save and restore her.

This didn't happen to me because I'm a pastor. (In fact, in this kind of situation, being a pastor is usually a liability.

When someone finds out what I do for a job, they clam up, start apologizing for their language, and change the subject—even their seat.) And this doesn't happen to me every time I take a plane somewhere. Usually my attempts to witness to my seat-mate end in awkward silence or the person putting on their noise-canceling headphones.

But every now and then—maybe one time out of ten—I find myself being used by God to do things I could never pull off on my own.

I've learned to live with the awareness that God is always at work around me, always sovereignly putting me in places to be his vessel. He never puts me anywhere by accident. You neither.

His unchanging plans are unfolding, and he might give us the privilege of being instrumental in how that happens. You don't need to be super-eloquent or know a ton of Bible verses. You just need to live with the awareness that our sovereign God has sovereignly put you into situations to see a problem, to believe his promises, and to release his power through prayer and obedience.

PREDESTINED TO PRAY

Reflecting on Exodus 32 in his sermon, David Platt put it this way: "When we pray, we take our God-given place and we use our God-ordained privilege to participate with God in the accomplishment of his purposes on the planet." Praying this way is not just a part of our Christian life; it's our primary calling. One of the reasons God saved you was so that you could pray. He appointed you to ask him for things he wanted to give.

A couple of years ago, we had a "Year of Prayer" at my church: a year when we saturated ourselves in God's promises to answer prayer. In preparation for that, I read a heap of books, and one that made a lasting impression was *A Gospel Primer for Christians* by Milton Vincent. In this book, Vincent looks at Ephesians 1:4: "He [God the Father] chose us in him [the Lord Jesus] before the foundation of the world, that we should be holy and blameless before him."

In his love, God chose us to be "before him": that is, to stand before him—to use our positions as beloved children to pray to him.

When we pray, we are fulfilling one of the primary purposes for which God saved us. This is why God put you and me here: to pray for what we see around us—to be his instruments to change destinies.

Christian, God has chosen you, as he chose Moses, to pray as part of his sovereign purpose. He's put you where you are right now so that you might look around and see the problems, and then enter his presence and say, "God, let your kingdom come here, let your promises come true in this place, and let your will be done in this moment."

It is because God's plans are unchanging that we pray with confidence and anticipation—because our prayers are part of the unfolding of that will. God's plans will happen—and, amazingly and awesomely, you can be a part of the way they happen.

Your prayers can change the world, just as Moses' prayers did. You just need to ask.

PART TWO

HOW TO
PRAY

CHAPTER FOUR

HOW *NOT* TO PRAY

Hopefully by now we have cleared up some of the biggest hindrances we face when it comes to praying. But the question remains: how are we supposed to actually do it?

When Jesus taught on this in his most famous message, "The Sermon on the Mount," though, before he gave his followers instruction about how to pray he warned them about how *not* to.

That's because everyone, regardless of their faith, prays. We've likely all heard the cliché "There are no atheists in foxholes." Almost all people, at some point, have called out to a higher power—whether that takes the form of a plea for help, a lament of contrition, or an expression of thankfulness. Jesus starts with the assumption that most people pray—and that most people pray wrongly. So in the lead-up to the "Lord's Prayer"—the most famous prayer of all time, and probably better titled the "Model Prayer"—he begins by addressing some of the most common ways that prayer goes wrong. Just as sometimes I have to say to one of my kids, "You do not speak to your mother like that," so God the Son knows he has to say to sinful, shortsighted and confused humans, "You do not speak to my Father like this."

Specifically, he tells us not to speak to God like the Pharisees—religiously orthodox Scripture people—or like the Gentiles—religious pagans. In other words, everybody will tend to get it wrong. No matter what your faith tradition, instinctively we all pray the wrong way.

It's not really surprising that the religious hierarchy hated Jesus so much when he came out with incendiary statements such as this one:

> *"When you pray, you must not be like the hypocrites [one of Jesus' favorite terms for the religious leaders. You can see why he made them mad]. For they love to stand and pray in the synagogues and at the street corners, that they may be seen by others. Truly, I say to you, they have received their reward." (Matthew 6:5)*

Jesus is saying, *Don't pray like these religious leaders, the ones who lead your prayer meetings. They are the last people you should model yourselves on.* What then, does "religious" prayer look like? And why does Jesus dislike it so much?

BEAUTIFUL, NOT USEFUL

First, religious prayers primarily seek to gain something from God rather than get close to God. They seek to use God. Specifically, Jesus calls out the tendency of the religious to use prayer as a way of feeling self-righteous. In first-century Jewish culture, religiosity meant respect: the more religious you were, the more respect you gained. So the guys in Jesus' sights here are choosing where they pray very carefully. They stand and pray aloud in the synagogues because that's where the people who will be most impressed by their praying are gathered. And they stand on the street corners too. Why the corners? Because that's where two streets meet, and so twice as many people will see and be impressed by them.

So prayer for this type of religious person is a means to an end—status with other people. Ironically, Jesus was saying what philosophers like Nietzsche, Marx, and Foucault would say in criticism of religion centuries later: that, for many people, religion is a means to power. It's a way of gaining influence over others. In first-century Israel, the more religious you were, the more important you were, and the more you were given respect, deference, and authority. This is using God—praying to get something from him.

God is no more a fan of being used as a means to an end than we are. Notice that Jesus says this kind of prayer gets literally nothing from God; the only "reward" for this kind of praying is the extra respect of a few people who don't really matter anyway. God, who is the only one whose opinion actually matters, is not involved. Prayers of this nature gain nothing from God—because, to put it bluntly, these people are not even really talking to him.

Here's a key difference between the prayer of a religious person and the prayer of a gospel person. The religious person prays to get something from God, but the gospel person prays to get more of God.

Imagine two different relationships. First, two men in business together. Because they have complementary skills, their business does really well. But they don't like each other very much. They stay together, though, because they make a ton of money. Their interactions, though frequent, are perfunctory, and they have little involvement in each other's lives. They don't hang out after work or spend time with each other's families. Their relationship is all business.

Now imagine a relationship between two people who have just fallen in love. They are totally infatuated with each other. Maybe you've been there or you're there right now. They spend hours talking. Not because their conversations net them income. They just love being together. They usually talk about, well, nothing, really. Their conversations are not aiming to work through an agenda or even reach a conclusion. They talk to one another because they love being together, not to get something from each other.

Religious prayer is business-like. Gospel prayer is personal. If God is simply useful to you—a means to an end—then you'll need to really discipline yourself to pray. You won't do it because you love it but because doing it gets something from God that you really want.

If God is beautiful to you, however, then you'll love to pray.

Let me illustrate this in one other way. In college, I signed up for a theater class, thinking we were going to do skits and learn improvisation. It turned out to be a class on the history of drama in the theater. We spent our entire semester learning about great plays. As a college junior, I was not interested in theater, so the class turned out to be a challenge. But I studied and did well in my theater class so that I could get a good grade. After all, good grades lead to good jobs, and good jobs lead to paychecks.

Now, 25 years later, I have a job. I have a paycheck. And guess what I enjoy doing? Going to the theater. In college, theater was a means to an end. I studied it only as a way to (eventually) get money. Now everything's flipped: I use money to enjoy theater. What was once a means has become an end. Theater used to be useful to me; now it is beautiful.

THE ACID TEST

Is God useful to you or beautiful to you? Do you seek him because he is a means to the good life or because knowing him *is* the good life? This really matters. If I pray to get something from God, then Jesus says—and we need to feel the force of this—that I'm a hypocrite. When he uses that word, Jesus doesn't have in mind what we usually think of when we think of a hypocrite—someone who is living a sordid double life: for example, in church on Sunday but running prostitutes throughout the week. Jesus here is speaking of someone who is super-religious but who does not seek God for God's sake. Someone who treats God as the way to get something else: a better life now, going to heaven when they die, a solid family, and so on.

In this passage Jesus is specifically warning against using prayer as a way to gain respect from others, but we can broaden the application of this principle to any number of things. Anytime we are more interested in what we can get from God than we are in God himself, we become a hypocrite.

This really challenges me. I know, for example, that I pray most fervently on Saturday nights. I confess my sin and make sure my life is clean. I avoid fights with my wife and try to be really nice to my kids. Why? Because I'm only hours away from preaching, and I really need God's help when I preach.

Is it bad to pray before I preach? Of course not. Should I feel a level of desperation for his help when I preach? Very much. But the fact that my prayer life takes such a dramatic step forward on that night of the week shows that my motivations are partially hypocritical: I pray mainly because God is useful to me as I preach. God is a means to the end of a good sermon. That's what I'm really after.

Every single one of us is susceptible to this. Maybe you find yourself mainly praying before big decisions. "God, please just show me your will." That sounds spiritual, but it's possible we're more concerned with God's will than with God himself. Maybe you find yourself praying before meetings, pitches, or taking tests—not so much because you want to know God and live out his will better, but because you want to land the order, win the project, or ace the exam. Or you pray for your kids' behavior. Again, that's a good thing. But is your motivation one of glorifying God or to make yourself look like a good, godly parent in church this Sunday?

So the question we need to pose to ourselves is this: is God useful to me or is he beautiful? Do I spend time with him because I have to or because I get to? Is my prayer a means to an end, or is a relationship with God an end in itself?

Jesus drives this point home by giving us an acid test. He asks, *Do you pray in secret?*

"When you pray," he says to his followers, "go into your room and shut the door and pray to your Father who is in secret" (Matthew 6:6). You see, the way to know your real motivation in prayer is to ask how much you pray when no one is watching—when you have nothing to gain from praying but greater fellowship with God. When what drives you to pray is mainly a desire to be close to God.

Augustine, writing in the 5th century, pointed out that nearly everything else that we do for God can be done for some reason other than love for God—to be seen by others, to be respected by others, to be praised by others, to fit in and belong with our family or our church, and so on.

But the only motivation that will lead us to pray in secret is that we love God. Prayer that no one else sees or finds out about is the one thing that you will do consistently if you simply want to know more of God because you love him.

So first, religious people pray to use God. *Don't pray like that,* Jesus says.

DON'T TRY TO IMPRESS GOD

The second thing Jesus warned about "religious" prayer is that religious prayers are offered with a sense that we need to impress God:

> "*When you pray, do not heap up empty phrases as the Gentiles do, for they think that they will be heard for their many words.*" (*v 7*)

Religious people think that in order for God to hear their prayers, they have to do something to gain his attention. So, they focus on long prayers, or loud prayers, or prayers uttered in just the right environment with the right phrases and the right accompanying sacrifices, as if God keeps a little account for you and will only answer your prayer when you get up to a certain amount.

But that assumes that God is basically hostile toward us, and therefore only if we say the right things in the right way, at the right volume and intensity, with the right degree of regularity, will he be impressed enough with us to be favorably inclined toward us. Prayer of this variety is about earning enough favor with the deity for him to like us and help us.

Most religions tend toward some version of this. For instance, I lived for a while among Muslims in Southeast Asia, and they would get together regularly to chant and pray the Quran. Once I was invited to go into somebody's house to be part of a prayer service asking for blessing on a house that had just gone through a tragedy. (I made clear that while they prayed to Allah, I would be praying to God the Father.) As we sat down in this house together, the Muslim leaders started chanting verses from the Quran, over and over again.

I sat patiently, waiting for it to end, but after an hour it dawned on me that that might not be any time soon. Over the course of that first hour, I had prayed in every way I could think of for this family as they dealt with this tragedy. Finally I turned to the guy sitting next to me and quietly asked, "How long does this go on?"

"Oh, I don't know—six or seven hours."

They assumed that to earn God's favor many words needed to be spoken. Evidently, it seemed, Allah likes words, and he won't do anything for you until you fill up his ears with pleasant phrases. If your "word count" with him is low, you shouldn't expect anything from him.

To be clear, this isn't just a problem with Islam. Catholics have their rosary beads and their Hail Marys. Buddhists have their chants. We Protestants can easily drone on and on in our prayers, bloviating with all sorts of formal, flowery language that we think unlocks the door to heaven, or in our worship choruses that repeat words again and again and again because we assume that by saying, "You are here, Lord" enough times, God will make it so.

The word translated "many words" is literally "babbling." It means praying with intensity and repetition—but not much meaning. If you think you need to pray until you earn God's attention, and then pray in a way that impresses God into looking favorably upon you, then that is how you will pray.

To this Jesus simply says, *Stop it.*

Not a lot of diagnosis or theological corrective. Just, *Cut it out. You don't understand the heavenly Father much at all.*

> "Do not be like them, for your Father knows what you need before you ask him." (v 8)

In other words, pray to a Father who you know loves you, is ready to receive you, and already knows what you need.

One thing I have noticed about young kids is that they are not shy in speaking with their parents. When my kids were little, if they wanted to talk to me, they would barge right on in, no matter what I was doing or who I was with. They always assumed that I had time for them.

And you know what? They were right.

Nothing brought me greater delight than seeing their bright eyes and smiling faces. They could approach me in ways that would have been disrespectful or rude if it had been anyone else. I remember years ago, when one of my daughters was three, we were doing an open-air baptism service. There were about 65 people lined up waiting, and there were maybe 200 people watching. It was mid-July in North Carolina, so it was baking hot. Then my daughter burst through the crowd like they weren't there, skipped the line, and ran up to me. She didn't hesitate. She didn't hang back. She didn't ask herself if maybe I was busy or pause to wonder what all those people were doing there. She had drawn a picture in her Sunday School class, and she wanted to show it to me. So she did. She assumed I'd want to see it.

And she was right.

My daughter did not feel she needed to impress me before she could approach me. She knew she could approach me because I loved her. So she came to talk to me in a way that for anyone else would have been rude.

This is how Jesus wants us to speak to God. That's why the first word of his "Model Prayer" is so revolutionary:

"Father."

No other religion had ever or has ever taught that. For his children, God is not a Judge that we need to placate but a Father who knows what we need and cares deeply for us. We don't need to impress him. We don't need to persuade him. We don't need to use the best phrases. We just need to talk to him as Dad.

Every other religion finds this bizarre, if not outright disrespectful. The Muslims I've known tell me they think the Christian view of prayer is irreverent. But that's kinda the point. It is so intimate that it does seem irreverent. And it would be, had God not offered this relationship to us himself. We would never have the confidence to pray like this had Christ not opened the way for us by paying our sin debt and giving to us his righteousness.

If you understand the gospel, you won't pray to impress God. Christ has already impressed God in your place. You couldn't add anything to Christ's finished work if you wanted to, and the good news is you don't need to. God already knows all about you. There's nothing that could be revealed about you that was not already paid for by Jesus. In Christ, there is nothing you could do that would make him love you more, and nothing you have done that would make him love you any less.

What Jesus wants us to see is that there is a specifically Christian way to pray. Christians pray with the awareness of God as their Father, who already knows them, loves them, and is aware of what they need. Their main driver in prayer is not to inform God about the needs in their lives that he's forgotten, or to curry favor with him, but to spend time with him.

A FEW NUTS AND BOLTS

I'll end this chapter with a little "dirty laundry" list of "don't do's" that I see creeping into the prayer practices of most Christians. I certainly see them in mine. (Of course, however inadequate our actual words are, God still loves to hear his children pray. If our words are a little clumsy, that's fine. It's just when they turn into habits that we might want to avoid them.)

First, don't keep repeating God's name in prayer as if repeating it more makes God hear you better. I'm not trying to be the grammar police here, but God knows you are talking to him; you don't have to keep reminding him. I have to imagine this gets a little annoying to God:

"Father God, I pray that you'd be with us today, Father God, and that you'd bless us, Father God, so that we can grow in love for you, Father God."

After all, I'd be annoyed if one of my kids came to me and, because they thought it would make me more likely to give them my attention, said:

"Father Dad, we just want you to be with us, Father Dad, and that you'd give us the new toy we want, Father Dad, and to protect us, Father Dad, so that we can be healthy and happy, Father Dad."

Second, perhaps we could ban the word "just" from our praying? Or at least call a small hiatus from it? "Lord, we just ask you to speak to us through your word" or "Father, we just ask you to heal this cancer."

Third, let's not ask God to do things he's already promised: "Just be with us." Boom. Hebrews 13:5.

Fourth, let's not use meaningless phrases with God. The one I love to hate most is "traveling mercies." What are those? Do they activate the moment I walk out the door, or only when I start my car? If I need, and can have, some special mercy while I'm traveling, shouldn't I have some "staying mercies," too? I'm just as likely to do something reckless or ungodly in my kitchen as on the highway.

Fifth, let's stop asking God to transmogrify our foods. It's good that we ask God to bless our meals before we eat. It really is. But what exactly are you asking God to do when you sit down to your 16-ounce, double bacon cheeseburger with onion rings, and you say, "God, bless this food to the nourishment of our bodies." We serve a God of miracles, but ordinarily he works through means; try putting something green on the plate before you offer that one up again.

Sixth, let's not use prayers to lecture people. Many small groups have some version of this overzealous preacher-posing-as-prayer-warrior kind of person. Their prayer is sort of praying, but really it's more lecturing and gossiping. It's "preach praying." "Lord, I beseech you to be with Rachel and her new boyfriend as they deal with purity. Lord, you called us to purity, and sometimes I see lust in their eyes and I see them holding hands, which they should save for marriage, Lord. So Lord, help them, please." I'll be honest: it happens at the front of church, too. "Father, we pray that you would bless us as we meet for our prayer meeting this Wednesday night, at 8pm, just in the other room, in our church fellowship hall. Lord, it's the most important meeting of the month, and I know it breaks your heart that so many of our people didn't come to the last one because of a basketball game. So would you move this church, at 8pm this Wednesday, to actually be committed to your mission, at 8pm this Wednesday, so they would overcome their idolatry of sports? Please cause all of these wayward sinners to walk in here, at 8pm on Wednesday. Amen."

I'm embellishing. But not much.

Finally, let's put some thought into the prayer requests we share with others. Am I praying with God's perspective and in line with God's stated purposes? I heard a while back about someone who had asked their small group to pray for their son, who was in the finals of a karate tournament. I appreciate them wanting God to be active in every area of their son's life, but what exactly were they asking their small group to pray? "Jesus, when Connor steps out onto that mat, would you just guide his foot into that other little boy's face? Lord Jesus, render his opponent unable to continue. Let little Connor's victory over him be definitive, decisive, and humiliating."

Full disclosure: I've prayed all those types of prayers. My instinct, like yours, is to pray religious prayers rather than gospel-based ones. Like a car severely out of alignment, the moment I stop thinking about the gospel, my prayer life veers into the ditches that Jesus warns about here—trying to impress God with my prayers or using them to manipulate him into giving me what I really want.

That's why I'm grateful that before Jesus teaches us how to pray, he warns us about ways not to pray—and it's why this chapter needs to be in this book. It sets us up to understand Jesus' really important instructions about how to pray, which is where we turn next.

CHAPTER FIVE

AMAZED
BY GOD

If you grew up in church, you'll probably have said the "Lord's Prayer" over a thousand times. Even if you didn't grow up in church, I'm guessing you can still complete the sentence, "Our Father, who art in heaven..." These are some of the most famous lines in the history of the world.

As I mentioned in the previous chapter, the "Lord's Prayer" is probably not the best name for this prayer. I prefer the "Model Prayer," because it is not so much an example of our Lord's personal prayer but rather his example to us for how to pray. (Just think—Jesus never had to ask God to "forgive us our debts.") If you are looking for how to pray, this is where you start. According to Jesus, our prayer times should follow this general pattern. I don't mean you merely recite the words—though that is not a bad place to start for, as Martin Luther said, this is a prayer that you can pray every day and always learn something new! But some of us have gotten so familiar with the words that we have lost the wonders they convey. And what wonders the words contain—this prayer embodies the essence of what it means to know and walk with God and encapsulates the difference between religion and relationship. And practically, it addresses another of our primary hindrances to prayer: I just don't know what to say!

In the next couple of chapters, we're simply going to walk through it line by line. Let me encourage you, if you haven't before, to memorize it. Then, as Tim Keller says, use the words of the prayer like a melody line that you "riff" off of in your prayer times. Jazz musicians play spontaneous, unique sequences of notes, inspired in the moment, but their note choices are neither arbitrary nor chaotic. They follow the melody line, called "riffing," which gives jazz music that distinctive originality and freshness while maintaining musical cohesiveness. The most rewarding prayer times I have come from riffing off the melody of the Lord's Model Prayer!

OUR FATHER IN HEAVEN

As we discovered in the previous chapter, this is the most revolutionary word of the prayer.

"Father."

The late theologian J.I. Packer said that you can measure someone's grasp of Christianity by how much they make of the fatherhood of God (*Knowing God*, page 226). From start to finish, he said, Christianity is an exploration and application of God's tender fatherhood in the life of the believer. So it shouldn't be a surprise that when Jesus, the Son of God, teaches us to pray, he starts there.

Here is a truth that should never fail to startle and stir us: we can approach the God of the universe as a beloved child and say to him, "Dad, I've got a need, and I need your help"—and the God of heaven, who made every star and who sustains every atom, not only stands ready to help but delights to listen. Why? Because he's our Father.

In *A Praying Life*, Paul Miller says that how we approach God in prayer demonstrates whether we really understand the gospel. See if you identify with this:

> *"When we slow down to pray, we're immediately confronted with how unspiritual we are ... In contrast, children never get frozen by their selfishness. They just come as they are, totally self-absorbed." (page 31)*

My kids have never come to me and said, "Dad, I have got something I really want to ask you for, but I just feel like my heart's not right as I'm asking this, and also I know that I haven't really been very loving and generous to my siblings today, so I'm thinking maybe I'll just stop right now and not talk with you for the rest of the day." No! They just blurt out what's on their minds, because they're my kids and I'm their dad, and they know that my acceptance of them is not conditional on their performance. The point here is not that sin should cease to grieve or sober us in the presence of God—as we'll see, confession and repentance should be a part of our prayer—but simply that we should not assume that only if we reach and maintain some standard of perfection will he receive us. He is always our dad, and he poured out his wrath toward sin once and for all on Jesus at the cross. The way is open; he welcomes us into his presence.

Many of us start our prayers with "Heavenly Father," but if you're like me, we don't often pause there long enough to realize the magnitude and the wonder and the glory of what we just said. We've already mentioned it several times throughout this book. But it's so central, so vital, so critical, that I don't want you to miss it: of all the titles that our sovereign, heavenly, holy God could command us to call him, it is not "Almighty One" or "Lord Conqueror" or "Exalted King" that he chooses. He says, "Call me Daddy."

If you get nothing else out of this book, get this one thing: that through faith in Jesus you have a place in God's family. Recognizing and reveling in the fatherhood of God is the engine of the Christian life.

If we don't grasp this, we'll live as spiritual orphans. We'll always be fearful that God's not listening, or that we've got to do one more thing to earn his attention and affection (to put it in Jesus' terms in Matthew 6, as "the Gentiles do"). There's a family at my church who adopted a number of children from a South Asian country. The mother shared with me that she often was saddened over how one of the little boys, who came into their family at the age of five, would try to manipulate, lie, and steal to get his way, rather than just asking her for what he needed. "I'm heartbroken," she said, "because he still thinks like an orphan fending for himself instead of the beloved part of the family we've made him to be."

You and I have been adopted into God's family. "See what kind of love the Father has given to us, that we should be called children of God" (1 John 3:1). Adoption is a one-time parental decision, not a conditional status that fluctuates with the behavior of the child. If you have accepted Christ, God has made you a part of his family, and that is final. Embracing the fatherhood of God imparts to you a confidence, and that enables you to pray through any temptation and trial. You don't need to come to God in fear or uncertainty, touting your goodness or twisting his arm. You need to come to him and simply say, "Father..."

My earliest memories of childhood involve me getting up early (5 am) and knowing right where my dad would be: in our living room, either on his knees or with a Bible open on his lap. I just assumed that he had always done that. One day, when I was older, he told me that he had not—for the first few years after he became a Christian (in his 20s) he simply couldn't motivate himself to pray. He always got up late and tired, and scrambled to get to work. He said he finally determined that he was going to get up 30 minutes earlier to have a prayer time if it killed him. He set his alarm appropriately for the next morning and asked God to help him get up when it went off. He woke up 15 minutes before his alarm went off, wide awake. He thought, "Well, God, I said help me wake up with the alarm—not this early!"

He told me that it was one of the times when he felt the Spirit of God impress something on him most clearly— the Spirit of God whispered, "I know, but I couldn't wait to get started."

My dad is one of the most consistent pray-ers I know— and this was the understanding that jump-started his prayer life. God your Father is excited about spending time with you. Prayer is not an obligation to fulfill; it is an invitation to find refuge in a loving heavenly Father.

Now, let me acknowledge something: I know that for some of us, that word "father" is complicated. You didn't have a good dad. He failed you. Neglected you. Abandoned you. Constantly criticized you. Abused you. If that's you, please hear me: I'm so, so sorry. I want you to know that none of that was God's design for your relationship with your dad. As you consider the difficult emotions and painful history that go with the word "dad," know that God is the first one to weep with you.

Here's what I want to encourage you to do, however: reverse the order of your comparison. Rather than seeing your heavenly Father through the lens of your earthly one, evaluate your earthly father through the lens of your heavenly one. You'll likely find it a very healing experience.

Maybe your earthly dad didn't care, and maybe he looked on you as more of a nuisance than anything else. Maybe he hurt and scarred you. That is not what fatherhood is meant to be. No—God shows you what fatherhood is meant to be. Your heavenly Father can't stop thinking about you. He exults over you constantly with singing (Zephaniah 3:17), and he's so attentive to you that he knows when even a single hair falls from your head (Luke 12:7).

Your earthly father may have done nothing for you, but your heavenly Father planned from eternity to save you at the cross so that you would not ever need to be alone.

Your earthly father may have been distant and played games with your affections and requests. Your heavenly Father invites you to go before him boldly and freely, even as he sits on the throne of the universe, to talk to him and to tell him what you need.

This is your Father. This is what fatherhood is meant to be. Embracing the love of your heavenly Father can help you come to peace with the failures of your earthly one. I'm not saying this will be a quick process, but in experiencing the fatherhood of God lies healing for a plethora of spiritual wounds. Our prayers are transformed when we begin by saying, "Our Father" because we are transformed in saying, and believing, those words.

HALLOWED BE YOUR NAME

"Hallowed": it's probably not a word you used in casual conversation yesterday. Or last week. Or maybe ever. I know a guy who grew up going to an old-fashioned church and who said that until he was eight years old he genuinely thought that God's name was Howard, because every week he solemnly intoned with the rest of the congregation, "Our Father, who art in heaven, Howard be thy name."

Ok, so presumably you know the difference between Howard and Hallowed—but what does "hallowed" actually mean? In this context, two things.

First of all, it means "most beautiful." When we say "Hallowed be your name," we are telling God (and reminding ourselves) that God is better than anything else, including anything else we are going to ask him for later in our prayers. We are saying that we are not going to give in to the temptation to treat God as a means to an end. We may be about to ask him to get us out of a fix, or give us healing, or help us with an exam or an interview or a presentation, or enable us to bear pain, or show us how to navigate a relational difficulty; and he's eager to help—but nonetheless we know that he is greater than any gift he may give us. So, in saying, "Hallowed be your name," we are saying, "God, I would love to have the new job. I would love to have a healed body. But God, you are better than any of those things, and if I don't get them, it's not going to affect my joy because you are my greatest possession. You are the one I hallow, the one I treasure."

As one of my favorite hymns, an old Irish hymn, puts it:

> Riches I need not, nor man's empty praise;
> Thou mine inheritance, now and always.
> Thou and thou only, the first in my heart;
> High King of heaven, my treasure thou art.

When we say "Hallowed be your name," we are saying, "My treasure thou art."

Second, "hallowed" means "most worthy." We are acknowledging that God's glorification is the loftiest purpose in the universe. My pleasure is not the point; his is. The point of my life is not to win glory for myself but to point people to him. The purpose of any requests I'm about to make is not (or at least, should not be) about prospering or promoting myself but about giving honor to his name. And that means that if God chooses to answer my request in a way that is not what I want so that he can get glory in another way, I'm saying that I'm ok with that.

In saying this, you are confronting yourself with the question: who or what is the main point of my life? Who is at the center?

Think of it this way: if your life were a movie, who would the main character be? Movies always have a major character or two and then a bunch of minor characters. What happens to the minor characters is less important than what happens to the major character. Often, they come onto the scene only to make a small contribution to the narrative of the major character. The plot, the tone, the conflict—everything—hinges on what happens to the major character, not the minor ones.

You might call this the "Lesson of Biggs Darklighter." I would guess that 97% of the readers of this book have no idea who Biggs is. But if you are a devoted *Star Wars* fan—the kind who owns your own light saber and dressed up as some extra-terrestrial to see the finale in the cinema—you'll probably know that Biggs was an X-Wing pilot in the first *Star Wars* film, *A New Hope* (1977), who shielded Luke Skywalker from getting shot. Because Biggs sacrificed himself, Luke was able to fire the shot that destroyed the first Death Star. We don't know much about Biggs—where he came from, who his friends were, what kind of journey led him to fly a starship and join the Rebellion, or what he hoped to do afterward—but without Biggs, the whole *Star Wars* saga would never have gotten off the ground. No successful rebellion, no reunion with Yoda, no Rey or Finn or Poe or redemption of Kylo, no happy ending in a galaxy far, far away.

But there is a happy ending, because of Biggs. Yet you've probably never heard of him. Why?

Because *Star Wars* is about Luke, not Biggs. And if we could talk to Biggs (which we can't, because—spoiler alert—he died, and because—extra spoiler alert—*Star Wars* isn't real), he would probably say that he doesn't care that we don't know him, because his small sliver of the story successfully served the purposes of the main character, Luke Skywalker.

In the story unfolding in our galaxy, you and I play roles similar to Biggs. We're not Luke. We may think of ourselves that way sometimes, but we're not. Jesus is.

Jesus is the one for whom this cosmos was made and the one whose name is most worthy of praise. If we get a walk-on part to serve his story in a way that helps others to "hallow" his name, our life will be a success.

We'll only pray correctly if we realize that the events of our lives are not about us, and this world is not here to serve us. "Hallowed be your name" is a way of telling God—and reminding ourselves—that it is his name, and not ours, that we want to be magnified.

God may hallow his name before others by prospering you, so that you can leverage your success to extend his kingdom and so you can give God credit for what he has given you in your life. But he might hallow his name by letting you suffer, so that you can show those around you in the midst of pain that you have joy in bad circumstances or in bad health, because he is more beautiful than health or wealth or anything else.

God is glorified when sick people get well. But he is also glorified when sick people suffer well, and even when they die well. The point for the believer is not whether they live or die, but that in all things they give glory to God.

Because God is most beautiful to us, and we recognize him as most worthy of praise, that enables us to say to him, with joy, "However my day goes and whatever you do with what I'm about to ask you for, Father, you are all I need, and your praise is what I most want—so, hallowed be your name."

YOUR KINGDOM COME, YOUR WILL BE DONE

By now, I hope you've recognized that the Model Prayer begins not with us asking God for anything, but with us telling God how great he is. It starts, in other words, with adoration rather than petition. That's because there is nothing that we really need more than to know God; and if we are not amazed by and satisfied by and enthralled by God, we will end up not asking for things correctly. We need to be dazzled by him more than we need anything from him.

So even having taught us to adore God, Jesus still doesn't get to the "give me" part of praying. He teaches us first to submit to God. That's verse 10:

> *"Your kingdom come, your will be done, on earth as it is heaven."*

When we say this, we are subsuming our agenda to his. Remember, prayer is not about getting God to further our plans so much as seeking to join God in his. This—the realization that our prayers are not for us to get God to help us with our agenda, but to ask him to let us help with his—revolutionizes a prayer life. We do not come to him asking him to help us build our little kingdoms of sand. We come to him asking him to build his eternal kingdom through us—to build it in us as we bring more and more of our life in line with his purposes. We come to him asking him to further his will, even where that is not the same as ours, because heaven's plans are always better than ours. After all, heaven is the place where God's will is perfectly done—and things are going a lot better there than they are here! We need to learn to say, "God, this is what I think I want, but your plans are always better."

Eugene Peterson points out in his book *Answering God* that the two phrases—"your kingdom come" and "your will be done"—are two sides of effective prayer. One is more proactive, asking God to change our messed-up situation by bringing his kingdom into it. The second part is more about surrender, telling God when we don't get what we want that his will is better. Peterson connects this to two different kinds of prayers in the Psalms: he calls these "morning prayers," in which you pray that God will use you to change your situation, and "evening prayers," in which you sweetly surrender to God's better will, knowing that, regardless of your circumstances, you can rest secure in his providential care.

Remember that the "Lord's Prayer" is intended as a template for our prayers. We don't pray each line and then say, "Amen" and go get on with our day, prayer time done. No—each line should function as a springboard for us to talk to God about the concerns which that line raises. We riff on it.

What is the best way to pray in line with "your kingdom come"—to riff in ways harmonious with that melody? First thing: pray Scripture. Pick up God's promises, his warnings, his invitations, and his commands as you find them in his word, and use them to pray. If we want to know what God wants to do in his world, we've already got a pretty detailed guide: the Bible. Praying Scripture is the way to pray for his kingdom to come.

To put it more bluntly, the prayers that start in heaven are the ones that are heard by heaven.

How far in line with God's stated purposes are your requests? Are your prayers centered on God's kingdom coming and his will being done? We know, for example, that God wants all people everywhere to repent and trust in Jesus. If God answered, in one fell swoop, every prayer you prayed last week, how many new people would be in the kingdom?

Mark Batterson says it this way: "Our most powerful prayers are hyperlinked to the promises of God" (*The Circle Maker,* page 93). I love that imagery. Our prayers have power when clicking on the words that would take us to a passage in the Bible. When we pray God's words back to him, we are praying prayers that really change things, as we saw in chapter 3. The Bible is a book of more than 3,000 promises. Don't leave even one unclaimed!

So don't just read your way through the Bible; pray through it. That's how it was written.

Here are three practical suggestions. First, start your day in God's word, highlighting things that stand out to you—promises, warnings, invitations, commands—and use those to jump-start your prayer time. One acronym we use at our church is HEAR:

Highlight things that stand out to you as you read.

Examine them to make sure that you are understanding them rightly. Use a Study Bible or commentaries.

Apply them by figuring out what difference they make in your life.

Respond to them by praying. Claim the promises. Ask for help.

Second, memorize God's word. I love listening to saints whose prayers are saturated with Scripture. One phrase from God's word bleeds right into another one—each phrase of the prayer hyperlinked to the Bible—so that, in effect, God is writing their prayers. That kind of prayer power doesn't happen by magic; it's the fruit of a lifetime of study. Carrying God's word around in our heads makes it easier for his promises to come alive in our hearts.

Even a little bit will go a long way. Set yourself a target of learning just two verses a month, every month. Even this will bring a revolutionary amount of energy, excitement, and confidence into your prayer life.

Finally, pray with the Spirit. The Holy Spirit is the one who is responsible for extending God's kingdom on earth (Acts 1:8): our Counselor in the execution of his mission (John 14:16). He is the one who knows the will of God (1 Corinthians 2:10b-12), and he is the one who helps us to pray, including when we don't have the words to speak coherently (Romans 8:26-27). So when we say, "Your kingdom come, your will be done," that is a request for the Spirit to make God's will known to us, in real time, and then to make it so through us.

Prayer is not only talking—it is a two-way conversation where there's some talking and there's also some listening as the Holy Spirit reveals what he wants for God's kingdom and what part he is calling us to play in building it. This means we need to develop the habit of listening prayer.

What I do not mean here is that we assume that every thought we have as we pray is the voice of the Holy Spirit, or that any promptings and focus that we receive in prayer carry anything like the authority of the word of God. Far more havoc has been wreaked in the world following the words "God told me to..." or "God told me you need to..." than with probably any other phrases! If you are going to announce "Thus saith the Lord..." then you need a chapter and a verse from the Bible to prove it.

Still, we need to acknowledge that God does speak to his people through his Spirit. There are 59 places in the book of Acts where the Spirit is mentioned. In 36 of those, he is speaking. But here's the thing: in each of those 36 encounters, the author of Acts never tells us exactly how he spoke. Did a bunch of people think the same thing at once? Did a little halo or thumbs-up emoji appear over the person of the head speaking? Alas, we're just not told. That ambiguity is intentional, I believe, not to frustrate us but to humble us. God doesn't want us to put the same level of certainty on what we *think* the Spirit is saying directly to us as what we *know* he is saying as we read our Bibles.

But while there may be mystery in knowing how he spoke, there is none about whether he spoke. His guiding voice is a constant presence in Acts.

Maybe you're saying, "Well, hold up. That was Acts. And they were apostles. It's not the same for us." I hear you. There certainly were some special things happening back then—the apostles had been charged, after all, with authoring the books of the New Testament (John 14:25-26). But there's nothing in Acts to indicate that the days in which the Spirit dynamically led Christ's church in the execution of his mission stopped with the apostles. In fact, I don't think you could convince me that the only book God gave us with stories from church history of what it looks like to walk with the Spirit is filled with a bunch of experiences of Christians that have nothing in common with us.

John Newton perhaps said it best. He asked how "that … which was so essential in the apostle's days, should be now so unnecessary and impracticable?" (*Select Letters of John Newton*, page 22).

So, while we need be wise in how we discern the Spirit's voice, we also need to beware of leaving him out of our prayer lives altogether. He supplies the power in our prayer. Paul says that he grants to many the gift of "faith" as they pray (1 Corinthians 12:9)—a supernatural insight into what God wants to do in a specific situation, accompanied by the confidence that he is going to do it. If you want your prayers to be powerful and effective, learn to pray with the Spirit, not just to the Father.

Practically, then, why not say to God as you pray, "God, I don't want to just pray to you today; I want to pray with you. Please, Spirit of Jesus, move in me as I pray. I'm not just here to talk; I want to listen also." Be led by the Spirit while taught by the word. It's truly exciting.

THE RIGHT PLACE TO START ASKING

Hopefully by now you're persuaded that Martin Luther was right—that there is a lot more in this short little Model Prayer than first meets the eye. And we haven't even gotten to the "ask me" sections yet!

Let that in itself be a lesson for us. Before we jump into what we need, we need to just stand amazed at who God is. Only then will we ask rightly. Effective prayer is more about posture than petition.

When we see God for who he is, and ourselves for who we are, then we will be ready to ask. And that's where we turn next.

CHAPTER SIX

ASK YOUR FATHER

I can't emphasize enough how important is the posture of chapter 5 in making the requests of chapter 6. But let's be honest, quite often we are driven to prayer by awareness of things that we need. And that's ok. I'd even say it's divinely orchestrated.

That's why the second half of the Model Prayer is a template for asking.

GIVE US THIS DAY OUR DAILY BREAD

Few of us think to ask God for literal daily bread since most of us know where our next meal is coming from. Sure, at times during 2020 we may have wondered where our next roll of toilet paper was coming from—but even then, most of us never truly worried about whether we'd eat that day. There are tragic exceptions, of course, but for most of us starvation is not a daily fear.

Many of us don't generally realize how uniquely comfortable our situation is. For most of our spiritual brothers and sisters around the world—and at many points throughout history—it makes complete sense to ask God for daily food. This request comes naturally to them, but it seems foreign to us. That's a blessing, but that comfort can delude us into something far more devastating: the sense that we can function as independent, autonomous, self-sufficient demigods.

Sooner or later life gives us a rude awakening. A microscopic virus comes along and destroys our way of life as we know it. One stock-market crash robs us of our fortunes. An unexpected call into your boss's office upends your plans for the future. The doctor's diagnosis turns everything upside down.

"Give us this day our daily bread" might be more relevant to us than we know, even if our pantries are stocked with supplies. "Give us this day our daily bread" is the recognition that day by day, moment by moment, we are to look to God for what we need to accomplish his will. In the Greek the phrasing here is literally "today bread"— and you might think of it as everything you need today to do whatever he commands.

It's worth asking, "Why use bread for the metaphor?" Jesus could have just said "provision." For most of history bread has been the basic foodstuff for most cultures. In asking for bread, we are saying, "God, I depend on you for even the most basic elements of life, not to mention the difficult ones."

Furthermore, in using "bread" Jesus was directing the minds of his Jewish hearers back to the exodus wilderness wandering. After God's people had been freed from slavery, they traveled through the wilderness on the way to the promised land, many miles from a Chick-fil-A, with nothing to eat. Every morning when they woke up, on the ground surrounding the camp was bread that tasted of wafers made with honey, which they called "manna" (meaning literally "what is it?"). That manna sustained the people of God every day for the forty years they were in the desert (Exodus 16). Each day it faithfully appeared, and each day they had enough. It was made into manna-bread and manna pudding and manicotti and everyone was happy.

But some Israelites struggled with the day-by-day-nature of the provision. God gave them strict instructions to gather only enough for each day—no stockpiling. The type-A people asked, *But what if there's a shortage? What if we're in a part of the wilderness that doesn't get much manna-fall? Having a safety deposit box of extra manna for a rainy day just seems like basic wisdom.* Yet when they stashed away some extra manna, God made it rot and breed worms (v 20-21). Why? Because trusting God for daily bread should be a day-by-day experience.

God wants us to do the same—so he teaches us to pray for our daily bread: for him to supply on that day what we need to do his will that day.

This is not telling us that we can't stock a pantry, stow money in a retirement plan, or plan ahead. But it does mean that day by day we look to God as the ultimate supplier of our needs. That means that when we're unsure of what the future holds and the next decade looks like a barren wilderness, we can trust that the God who supplies us today will take care of us tomorrow, too.

MORE THAN JUST BREAD

Jesus is, then, clearly talking about more than bread here. In Jesus' famous confrontation with Satan, which took place right before this sermon, he declared to Satan,

"Man shall not live by bread alone, but by every word that comes from the mouth of God" (Matthew 4:4). The human body is fueled by bread, but the human soul needs bread of a different kind. We need God's wisdom, strength, and daily supply of grace in our lives.

Your daily bread is whatever you need to accomplish the task God has called you to. He will supply you with the wisdom you need to parent. With the guidance you need to make good decisions. With the strength to endure temptation. With the grace to make it in marriage or in singleness. With the words for being an effective witness. Anything you need to fulfill the tasks God has given you, he will supply.

Paul tells us not to be anxious about anything, but in everything to make our requests known to God (Philippians 4:6). Nothing in our life need cause us anxiety because we are allowed to pray about everything, and our all-sufficient, infinitely generous God will daily give us everything we need for everything we face.

Not long ago I went through Scripture and made a (non-exhaustive) list of the kinds of things people prayed for. Many of the requests I found were spiritual—the kind you might expect. But a lot of them were very practical. Here's a handful, in no particular order:

Hannah prayed for a son (1 Samuel 1).

Solomon prayed for wisdom (1 Kings 3).

Manoah asked God to show him how to raise his son (Judges 13:8).

Eliezer prayed that he would meet the right girl to introduce to his BFF Isaac (Genesis 24).

Joshua prayed for the sun to stand still to have more time to get the job done (Joshua 10:12-13).

David prayed for help in trouble (Psalm 86:1-2).

Hezekiah asked God to turn back an invading army (2 Kings 19:15-19).

Daniel asked God to show him the meaning of a dream (Daniel 2:3, 17-19).

Jacob prayed for God to keep him safe from his angry brother (Genesis 32:6-12).

Gideon prayed (twice) for God to confirm something he was calling him to do (Judges 6:36-40).

Elijah prayed that it wouldn't rain (James 5:17).

And then he prayed that it would (James 5:18).

Nehemiah asked God to give him the guts to make a big request of his boss (Nehemiah 2:4).

A desperate dad prayed for his dying daughter (Mark 5:21-43).

Paul prayed that he'd be able to go and see his friends (1 Thessalonians 3:9-13).

The early church prayed for boldness in the face of persecution (Acts 4:24-30).

John prayed for Jesus to return (Revelation 22:20).

I could go on. Throughout the Bible, you find people praying about anything that matters to them: anything that seems essential to doing what they think they're supposed to do. Just like God wants them to.

Here's a truth that took me far too long to learn: if it matters to you, it matters to God, and so you can pray about it. And when you do, "the peace of God, which surpasses all understanding, will guard your hearts and minds in Christ Jesus," because we know that no good thing will be withheld from those who walk uprightly in trusting God (Philippians 4:7; Psalm 84:11-12). We need to learn to what David knew about God: that "those who know your name put their trust in you, for you, O LORD, have not forsaken those who seek you" (Psalm 9:10).

I have been disappointed by all kinds of people in my life. Most of all I have been disappointed by that rascal J.D. Greear. But God has never disappointed me. He has never let me down. So I can say, "God, please provide me today with what I need. I am not going to be anxious, for you will give me what I need to accomplish every good work that you have prepared for me to do today. If it's bread I need, it's bread you'll supply. If it's energy, or insight, or courage, or health, or meeting someone, or even the sun standing still—you'll supply it."

Here's Paul Miller again: "Learning to pray doesn't offer us a less busy life. It offers us a less busy heart. In the midst of our outer busy-ness, we can develop an inner quiet" (*A Praying Life*, page 23).

We develop that inner quiet by remembering that the God who provided miraculous manna in the wilderness day by day is perfectly able and willing to give us whatever he knows we need today. And then to do the same tomorrow. And then the day after that. So we should eagerly pray each day, "Give us this day our daily bread."

FORGIVE US OUR DEBTS

"Forgive us our debts" is not a throwaway "I know we're all sinners and make mistakes so don't judge me" kind of line. It reminds us that when it came to the greatest need we have—forgiveness—our generous Father made provision even for that, even at great cost to himself. (You could argue that many of our needs God can supply with no effort at all—he can take five loaves and two fish and multiply them into a meal for 5,000 with the sweep of his hand.) To purchase our forgiveness required the gory sacrifice of his Son on the cross. And still he willingly and lovingly supplied forgiveness.

Praying this phrase also reminds us that forgiveness is something we require continually. Sin is like a debt that accumulates every day. We must never forget that it is Christ's finished work, and not our own performance, which means that we can enter eternity with God and enjoy his love forever. We may have accepted God's love once for all at conversion, but its benefits are reapplied to us day by day.

Every day our hearts should sing:

> *Jesus paid it all,*
> *All to Him I owe;*
> *Sin had left a crimson stain,*
> *He washed it white as snow.*

Theologically, I get this. In practice, though, I tend to want to skip over this part of the Lord's Prayer. On any given day, I can think of a lot of "bread" that I need God to give me. It takes a lot more discipline to identify the sins that I need God to forgive through the blood of Jesus. At other times, when I can call up my sins, it is easy to get stuck in a cycle of shame and forget that God has forgiven me, fully and finally, through the blood of his Son Jesus.

To put it another way, it's possible to think too highly of yourself, so that you don't think you really need forgiveness—which is blind pride; or to think too lowly of yourself, so that you don't believe that God has really forgiven you—which is unbelief.

That is why we need this line: "Forgive us our debts." It reminds us that, as a great modern hymn puts it, "our sins, they are many," and that "his mercy is more."

Again, remember that this prayer is a template. When we reach the word "debts," we should identify ours specifically. Confession is an important, though much-neglected, part of the Christian life because it helps us clear out sin so that it does not grow and spread in us; and it moves us to be aware of just how wide and deep and astonishing is the mercy of God.

When we confess our sin, it loses its power over us. Sin is like mold, which thrives in the dark but not in the light. When we name our sin before the Lord, acknowledging that there is no excuse for it—that it is not just a "mistake" or a "lapse in judgment" but a willful, sinful corruption so bad that Jesus had to die to eradicate it—then the power of sin is broken. Expose your sin to Jesus, and he will forgive it. Seek to cover it, and it will destroy you.

I struggle with confession. It's not that I live under the illusion that I am perfect, but I hate naming my sins. In fact, when I pause to confess, I usually can't think of anything. It's as if my psyche conspires against me to keep my faults hidden. To help me with it, a mentor told me to ask my wife to identify those places in which I struggle most consistently and write them down in my journal. Asking her might have been a rookie mistake. It was like a question she'd spent years preparing to answer. She rattled things off so fast I couldn't keep up; eventually, I asked her to help me narrow it down to five or six major categories. Seriously, though, I now try to review those categories periodically, asking the Spirit to call to mind specific ways that I've gone wrong in them. And, over the years, he has led me to still other areas that weren't even on my mind when I began.

Confession grows our love for Jesus because the more we understand the depth of our sin, the more we appreciate the height of his love. The great early-19th-century English preacher Charles Simeon called it "growing downwards"—humbling ourselves again and again before the Lord, so that we are brought nearer and nearer to the foot of the cross to say:

My sins, they are many—Your mercy is more.

Those who are forgiven much love much (Luke 7:47).

... AS WE ALSO HAVE FORGIVEN OUR DEBTORS

As hard as confession itself is, the standard to which Jesus tells us to hold ourselves may be even more challenging: "Forgive us our debts," he teaches us to say, "as [in the same manner that] we also have forgiven our debtors."

An awareness of how deeply we've been forgiven should create compassion in our hearts toward others. If that kind of generous grace doesn't abound in our hearts, we have good reason to question whether we've experienced

God's grace. How could we know we've been forgiven of so much and be so unforgiving toward others? Right after giving us this model prayer, Jesus even adds, "If you do not forgive others their trespasses, neither will your Father forgive your trespasses" (Matthew 6:15). It's not that Jesus is overturning the whole "salvation by grace through faith" teaching and saying that the work of forgiving others is now a precondition for salvation. He's simply saying it is impossible for someone to have any real concept of God's extravagant grace toward them and not become gracious towards others. Your forgiveness, your generosity, your empathy toward others is an acid test that demonstrates whether you have actually experienced the grace of God.

The power to forgive can't just be willed into existence by the human heart. It can't be commanded any more than you can command a hungry man to feel full. The power of forgiveness is only unlocked in our hearts by the truth of the gospel. When I think God blesses me because I deserve his blessing, I'll be fine with giving to people what I think they deserve. Those who have hurt or disappointed me, or who have failed to live up to my standards, don't deserve my kindness. When I look at another person's sin against me and think, "I would never do anything like that," I will very likely withhold my forgiveness from them. But when I realize I have done the very same things to God, and so much more, forgiveness begins to become as natural to my soul as breathing.

The gracelessness of so many professing Christians shows that many have likely never experienced the power of the gospel. It does not matter how "Christian" you look or sound, how many Bible verses you know, how much you do in ministry, or for how long you have been a member of a church. If you don't recognize that the debt of yours that God canceled is greater than any offense against you—if you won't forgive others because you don't appreciate how much God has forgiven you in Christ—then you need to ask very seriously whether you are a Christian at all.

I am not saying that believing the gospel makes forgiveness easy; but I am saying that it makes it possible. As we reflect on the forgiveness we have received for the sins we have committed, we're transformed and freed to forgive others. I learned this in the early years of my marriage. Veronica is awesome—unquestionably God's greatest earthly gift to me—but, like me, she is a sinner. And because of that, on occasion she has hurt and disappointed me. When we first got married, my response to those occasions was to be angry and unforgiving toward her—because I felt I deserved to be treated better.

Then one day a friend pointed out to me that my own life was characterized by the same selfishness that I was mad at in her, and that I had disappointed and failed God far more than Veronica had disappointed and failed me—and that God nevertheless accepted me, forgave me, and was kind to me. And in that moment—yes, I can remember the exact moment—my heart softened. In fact, I think it saved our marriage. I realized that I needed to say, "I won't give to my wife what she deserves, and I'll pray that she won't give me what I deserve, because God has not given either one of us what we deserve. Instead he's given us the blessing that we don't deserve." The gospel was establishing a culture of grace in our marriage, and that is what saved it and strengthened it.

In saying this, I am not saying that forgiveness means that you don't confront and address the wrong, or that you shouldn't seek justice where legally appropriate. I am certainly not saying that it means remaining in an abusive situation where you or your loved ones are in harm's way. Rather, I am saying that we are not to harbor unforgiveness: to hold grudges and feed resentment. Ironically, doing so actually keeps us more tethered to those who have hurt us. Forgiveness, in other words, begins to break the bonds that others have put on us. Forgiveness is freedom.

Forgiveness is not easy; but the gospel makes it possible. When we see forgiveness less as a requirement for blessing and more as a grace first given to us in Christ, we can forgive freely, deciding, as Tim Keller puts it, not to bring up that wrong with the person, with others, or in our own thought—"not to dwell on the hurt or nurse ill-will toward the other" (*Judges For You*, page 191). That can only happen when you are in awe of what God has done for you.

So, don't miss the promise as well as the challenge in the words Jesus teaches you to say to your Father: "Forgive us our debts, as we also have forgiven our debtors."

LEAD US NOT INTO TEMPTATION, BUT DELIVER US FROM EVIL

Here's a painful and humbling truth: left to myself, my love for God would shrivel up and any flicker of divine life would go out. Scripture is not flattering in regards to our "natural" state (that is, our state apart from the active working of God's grace in us):

• Apart from grace, we would not seek the things of the Spirit of God. They would seem like foolishness to us (1 Corinthians 2:14).

- Apart from grace, our hearts are deceitful, and our desires are bent towards selfishness and sin (Jeremiah 17:9; James 1:14-15).

- Apart from grace, we would not recognize Jesus as Lord (1 Corinthians 12:3).

- Apart from grace, we would not even desire to do God's will (Romans 8:7; Philippians 2:13).

- Apart from grace, Paul says, "nothing good dwells in me" (Romans 7:18).

- Apart from grace, God's verdict on each of us is: "None is righteous, no, not one; no one understands; no one seeks for God. All have turned aside; together they have become worthless; no one does good, not even one" (Romans 3:10b-12). The word "all" in Greek means just what it does in English: no exceptions.

That means that without the active work of the Holy Spirit in us, we would all go astray, even knowing what we now know. According to Scripture, our sinful flesh, which stays with us until we die, is like a car severely out of alignment. As long as our hands are firmly on the wheel, we may be able to keep the car going straight down the road. But it takes a lot of effort, and if we take our hands off the wheel for even a moment—guiding it along with our knee, for instance, while we eat a burrito—the car immediately lurches towards the side of the road. Like moths to the flame, we veer toward evil. As the hymn-writer Robert Robinson put it, "Prone to wander, Lord, I feel it, prone to leave the God I love."

So we need to pray for ourselves, for our families, and for our churches, "Father, lead us not into temptation, but deliver us from evil." "Temptations" are the wickednesses that come from inside of us. "Evil" is the attacks of our enemy from the outside, which cater to our temptations. Literally we should pray every day, "Keep me from myself, Lord. Restrain me lest I run straight after sin, Father. If you take your Spirit from me for one second, I'll spiritually implode." With Robert Robinson, again, we pray, "Here's my heart, Lord, take and seal it; seal it for thy courts above."

The longer I go in ministry, the more convinced I become that even the best of us are "prone to wander." I'm reminded of that when I consider how many of the ministry friends that I started out with are no longer in ministry, some having left their wives and some not even following Jesus. If eight years ago you'd asked me to name the top ten most influential young pastors in the US, I would have given you a list that today would have more than half the names crossed off. I shudder at just writing that. Five of those men are no longer in ministry, and not because God called them to exciting pursuits elsewhere. No, these men had huge churches, thriving ministries, best-selling books—but they were morally disqualified by egregious abuses of power, covetousness or immorality.

Why? After all, they seemed to be better men than me—better preachers, more gifted ministers, more inspiring leaders. Many showed a resolve in leadership and strength of character that I lacked. Why did they fall?

I asked Dr. Paul Tripp, a very well-known counselor, pastor, and author, who knew several of these fallen leaders personally. He said he noticed two consistent patterns in their lives:

First, they had become separated from authentic (and local) community and from true peer relationships—that is, from people who could look them in the eye and say, "That's bad, and you need to change."

Second, he said, they forgot the power of indwelling sin, which made the lack of peer community lethal. They forgot that just because you are spiritually "mature"... just because you're a pastor... just because your ministry is fruitful... it doesn't mean that you are not a sinner, with nothing good dwelling in your flesh. They had not remembered Paul's warning: "Let anyone who thinks that he stands take heed lest he fall" (1 Corinthians 10:12)— and so sin had overcome and destroyed them. They had stopped saying daily to God, "Father, lead me not into temptation, and deliver me from evil—because if you don't, I will self-destruct."

I don't want to follow their trajectory, and daily heeding Jesus' admonition to plead with the Father to deliver me from the evil within and the evil from without helps me stay vigilant.

We need to be sober-minded, but we don't need to be discouraged. Gloriously, God has promised that he will deliver us as we ask him to. "God is faithful, and he will not let you be tempted beyond your ability, but with the temptation he will also provide the way of escape, that you may be able to endure it" (1 Corinthians 10:13). God never puts us in a position where we have to give in. He never puts us in a situation where there is no way out or where his grace is not sufficient for the challenge. He will provide a way of escape. Always. No matter how overwhelming a temptation may feel, our Father always puts a backdoor in there through which we can run. He died to save you from the penalty for sin, and with that finished work comes the ability to live obediently.

AMEN!

This prayer is not just showing us how Jesus wants us to pray (though it does primarily do that); it's a glimpse into how he, too, prayed during his lifetime. He called God his Father. He prayed that his Father would glorify his name (John 12:28). He prayed that his Father's will would be done. He prioritized the Father's kingdom. He asked his Father for daily provision. He had no need to ask for forgiveness, but he asked for it for others (Luke 23:34) and then offered himself to secure it for them. He relied on the Spirit's guidance to resist temptation (Matthew 4:1).

And the Father responded to him every time he prayed these things—except for in one twenty-four hour period. In the Garden of Gethsemane, three times he called out to his Father only to be met by silence (Mark 14:35-41). And so, as he hung on the cross, for the first time in his life—and the only time in the New Testament—he addressed God without calling him Father: "My God, my God, why have you forsaken me?" (Mark 15:34).

The Father forsook Jesus once, during that dreadful hour of trial, so that you and I could be forever accepted by him. The Father turned his back on his Son so that he could smile upon us. He refused to deliver his Son from evil, letting him suffer the full force of it so that we could be delivered from it. Because the Father turned a deaf ear to Jesus in that moment, we can be assured that he hears us, and that he will bring us into his kingdom, will bring his kingdom to others through us, will forgive us, will deliver us from evil, and will provide all the bread we'll ever need.

Jesus not only taught us how to pray; he made effective prayer possible. Prayer is a conversation between a child and their loving Parent, and that was made possible through the death of Jesus.

When we understand that, we adore. We submit. We rest.

We ask.

CHAPTER SEVEN

ON PRAYING FOR GUIDANCE

G *od, should I take this job?*

Should I go out with him?

Should I break up with her?

Do you want us to relocate?

What school should I go to?

How should I respond to this opportunity?

God, show me the way!

Lots of requests on my prayer list have changed over the years, but one has stayed the same—the request for guidance. At any given moment, the greatest stress-producer in my life is uncertainty over what I'm supposed to do next.

I bet you can relate. One of the main sources of tension in our lives is looking for, waiting on, and praying for God's guidance for our lives. How to discern God's will is the number one question I get asked at events for young adults with an open Q&A.

However, up until about a half-century ago, guidance was not a huge issue for the Christian. Search the archives of the old Puritans from the 1500s and 1600s, who wrote pages and pages on every facet of the Christian life, and you'll find scarcely a mention!

I think that's because 21st-century life contains so much choice—so much more than our grandparents and great-grandparents had; and these choices are advertised to us as defining moments—with the right choice leading us toward blessing and the wrong one to doom. Perhaps we've gone from neglect to obsession.

It reminds me of reading those old "Choose Your Own Adventure" books. Do you remember those? I loved them. And I hated them. I was the one making the choices about what the main character did as I read the book, and so the story was in my hands. But the books were tricky. When you encountered a witch outside the cave, you might think the right choice would be to bolt—"If you want to run away from the witch, turn to page 47"—but then you turn to page 47 only to learn that in running away, you tripped and fell into the mouth of a volcano. (Pro-tip: I ended up finding the "right ending" on the final page and then reading the book backwards from there. I can't have been the only one.)

Unfortunately, real life doesn't work like that. Just recently I watched the show *You vs. Wild* starring Bear Grylls, an interactive TV show in which you choose what Bear will do to survive in the wilderness. My choices led to him being emergency evac'ed by helicopter. It didn't leave me with much confidence when it comes to guiding myself.

Furthermore, it seems that being a Christian only heightens, rather than alleviates, the tension. Because these choices feel so consequential, "finding God's will" feels to us like some kind of guarantee that ensures we will avoid disaster, achieve our dreams, and be able to live our best life now. And if we miss his will? Well, you might as well turn to page 47 and find your volcano, right?

To be clear, the Bible is clear that the Spirit does guide God's children. (We'll get to the biblical examples of that in just a minute.) But the million-dollar question is *how* he guides us.

Do you wait for a tingly feeling while you pray that indicates "door number three"? Or do you wait for a weird circumstance to show up in your life that you just know has to be God's signpost? A friend of mine who grew up as a pastor's kid told me about a time when his dad was facing a really major life decision. They were driving home discussing the choice, and as his dad pulled into the driveway he was presenting the positives of one of the options when a bunch of birds took off from their yard. His dad said, "Son, this is a sign from God. Those are seven doves. Doves are Jesus' favorite animal. And seven is the number of completion. So now we know what God wants."

My friend said he chose not to quibble with his dad, but he was pretty sure it was a passel of pigeons, not a flight of doves.

We might shake our heads smugly at such a story, but I'll bet you can think of at least once or twice when you've done something similar. An odd set of coincidences made us ask if God was trying to say something to us. Pigeons, doves, wet fleeces (Judges 6:36-40), warm fuzzy feelings, an emotional feeling in worship—which is the voice of God?

I'm going to lead you through a favorite psalm of mine that has helped me, because it contains a promise of guidance and hints about how it all works.

Here is the promise: God will "instruct [you] in the way that [you] should choose" (Psalm 25:12). In the rest of the psalm, the writer, King David, touches on decisions regarding relationships, calling, health, and parenting, believing God's promise for each of these. Those are the issues about which he's going to ask God, "Teach me your paths" (v 4).

Counterintuitively, as Tim Keller puts it, the big question of Psalm 25 is not how God guides, however, but whom God guides. Before we ask, "God, show me which way to go," King David wants us to look at ourselves and ask, "Am I the kind of person God shows which way to go?"

He then lays out for us four key characteristics of the person who receives the guidance of God.

TRAINED IN HIS WAYS

First, the person who gets the guidance of God is the one trained in the ways of God: "Make me to know your ways, O Lord" (v 4), and then "Lead me in your truth and teach me" (v 5). David is talking about an inward familiarity with the ways of God that causes him instinctively to desire the things in which God delights.

Think of this as similar to the way an athlete trains. A coach cannot train an athlete in how to respond to every possible game situation. What they can do, however, is hone in the athlete the instincts necessary to read situations rightly and respond to them successfully. I once heard a post-game interview with Michael Jordan, the greatest basketball player of all time (no disrespect to LeBron, but the last dance belongs to Michael). After a game in which Jordan had done some amazing, acrobatic dunk, a reporter asked, "Mr. Jordan, do you plan dunks like that in advance?" Jordan's response was "Not really. I just usually jump and decide in the air."

He's describing instinct. Jordan didn't have to look to the side of the court for his coach's advice. He just reacted. Correctly.

Now, that doesn't mean just anyone could do that. I have tried many times to "jump and decide in the air," and it rarely turns out well. Usually it involves a charging foul and sometimes hospitalization. Jordan looked like a bird in flight. I look like a wounded duck coming in for a crash landing.

But at the same time, while Jordan's acrobatics looked spontaneous, they were actually the fruit of instincts honed through hours of practice.

That is similar to what David is talking about here— spiritual instincts that discern what God wants without having it spelled out. The writer of Hebrews talks about those "who have [had] their powers of discernment trained by constant practice to distinguish good from evil" (Hebrews 5:14). How does he say that happens? By chewing on the "solid food" of Bible teaching.

These believers, the writer of Hebrews says, have moved beyond the spiritual "milk" that infants require: that is, simple and explicit instructions about exactly what to do in every situation. Toddlers need clear instructions and constant supervision lest they stab the fork into a wall socket. The writer of Hebrews envisions something better for mature believers—knowing the ways of God so well that when you are in a situation where the Scripture does not tell you definitively, *This is evil; don't go this way* or *This is good; do go this way* or *Turn to page 68, not page 47,* you can still tell what God wants.

So, if you want God to guide you, get so saturated with Scripture that discerning the ways of God becomes instinctive. As another psalmist says, you will never live out the will of God more than you know the word of God (Psalm 119:9).

Oftentimes, knowing the Scriptures keeps you from having to ask, "God, which way should I go?"—because you already know. In fact, if you are asking God to show you the way without bothering to learn the Scriptures, you're already dismissing God by refusing to avail yourself of the primary tool he has given you for discerning his will.

OBEDIENT TO HIM

Second, the person God guides is the one who is obedient to him. That may seem obvious, but there's a sequence here that's easy to mess up.

David promises,

> "He leads the humble in what is right and teaches the humble his way. All the paths of the LORD are steadfast love and faithfulness, for those who keep his covenant and his testimonies." (Psalm 25:9-10)

Humility means knowing that God's way is best, even when it isn't the way we'd have preferred. When we are walking in humility, we are obeying God in every way we know how.

The prerequisite to guidance for the next step is obedience in the present one. God's promise to give guidance in an area that Scripture does not address directly is given to those who are obeying him in those areas that the Scriptures do clearly address. If I pray for God's wisdom and leading in some decision over here where it's not clear what I should do, while at the same time I'm living in defiance to God's clear command in this other area over there, then I need to stop talking to him about that decision until I have dealt with my disobedience. You can imagine God saying, *I'm not going to tell you about what I haven't addressed in my word when you are not obeying what I have said in my word!*

So don't pray about whether to bid on a particular house while you're living with someone you're not married to. Don't pray for a promotion or a raise if you're not obeying God's command to be generous in your current position and with your current pay. If you are deliberately, continually disobeying God in some area, that suggests that you don't trust him to guide your life. James tells us that a person with that posture will not receive any guidance from God (James 1:7).

Do you want God's guidance? Live obedient to those things God has revealed. Seek humbly to obey his decrees. Obedience may lead you to some surprising and unwanted places, but you'll know he'll be there to protect and sustain you. Even when he leads you through the valley of the shadow of death, you'll have the assurance that he is with you, and that with his rod he protects you and with his staff he guides you (Psalm 23:4).

TRUSTING IN HIS PROMISES

Third, the person whom God guides is the one who trusts his promises. "No one who waits for you will be disgraced" (25:3, CSB). "Waits" means that we are in a place where we cannot yet see God's promises being fulfilled—in fact, we may be unsure how they could ever be fulfilled.

The necessity of faith is a recurring theme in regard to answered prayer. The one who receives guidance is the one who was already trusting that God would give it, just as he promised.

Candidly, I don't like waiting. Waiting is not something I do well. I like action. Result. Verification. But waiting in confidence is the essence of faith. The one who receives guidance is the one who was confident that God was going to give it, just as he promised: "The LORD is good to those who wait for him, to the soul who seeks him" (Lamentations 3:25).

David assures us in this psalm: "The secret counsel of the LORD is for those who fear him." That phrase, "secret counsel," implies that there are things that God shares only with those who seek to stay close to him. In a sermon preached at Redeemer Presbyterian Church, Tim Keller said of this verse, "This phrase points to special moments of guidance that the Spirit of God sometimes gives" ("Disciplines of Guidance," February 9, 1997).

What does that "Spirit guidance" feel like? Well, that's a big question, and I wrote a whole book about it called *Jesus Continued...*, but here's a short answer.

Sometimes, the Spirit speaks through the church. For example, Acts 13:2 says, "The Holy Spirit said [to the church], 'Set apart for me Barnabas and Saul for the work to which I have called them.'" Notice that God had something for Barnabas and Saul (Paul), but he didn't tell it directly to them—he told it to the church. Many times in my life God has raised up a brother or sister from the church with a word of encouragement, guidance or warning just when I needed it. If you are disconnected from the church, you have cut yourself off from a crucial component of God's guidance.

Sometimes, the Spirit guides through an inner prompting, a supernatural revelation, a divine gifting or an unshakable burden. Nehemiah knew that God wanted him to go and rebuild the walls of Jerusalem—but read the whole book and you will never find even one time when God tells him in audible words that this is what he wants him to do. All we are told is this: "God had put [rebuilding the walls] into my heart" (Nehemiah 2:12). The Spirit gave Nehemiah a burden, a desire, a passion that Nehemiah sensed had to be from him. Some of us will experience a passion for a particular ministry, or for Jesus to be made known in a particular place, and we will recognize as we pray about it that this is a prompting of the Spirit of God. But there's no shortcut to that. The secret counsel comes to those who fear the Lord—those who are trained in his ways and who are committed to obeying him.

Still other times, the Spirit guides through his sovereign control of circumstances. In 1 Corinthians 16:3-9, Paul lays out his plans like this (my paraphrase): *When I arrive in Corinth, I'll see what everyone thinks about me going on to Jerusalem. I tried to get Apollos to come visit you, but he didn't think it was a good idea to do it now. For now, my plan is to come to you after I go through*

Macedonia. I'll probably stay awhile, maybe even through the winter. I want to take my time, if the Lord permits. I'm also going to spend some time in Ephesus because there seem to be some great things that God is doing there. Kevin DeYoung, in a great little book called *Just Do Something,* makes this comment:

> "*You don't get the sense that the apostle got angelic visits every other day and waited for his dreams to tell him what to do.*" *(page 68)*

Sometimes, it's both—the Spirit uses both circumstances *and* supernatural promptings to guide. In Acts 16:6-7, for instance, Paul and his mission team attempt to go preach the gospel in Asia, but the Spirit won't let them. So they head for Bithynia, and again the Spirit closes the door. Some of this was circumstantial—Paul physically couldn't get there. And then in verse 9, Paul gets a dream of a man calling him to Macedonia—so they go there, and the churches of Philippi, Thessalonica, Berea, Athens, and Corinth are founded. That was a very clear inner prompting following a very confusing period of circumstantially closed doors.

Ok, you say, but what does that mean in the moment that I actually need to make a decision? It means that when it's time to make the decision, take advantage of every resource for guidance that God has put at your disposal. Search the Scriptures and listen to God. Lean on every bit of wisdom. Seek out counsel from your church (which means you are actually inviting them to speak into your decision). Pray. Draw up a list of pros and cons. Assess your own giftings. Consider the circumstances.

Then make the decision and trust that God has supplied all that you needed to make it, that if you needed more input he'd supply it, and that if you have missed something, then, like a good shepherd, he'll gently correct your path.

That makes it sound easy, doesn't it? Maybe you feel like it's got to be harder—or at least more mystical—than this? The truth is, we usually make this a lot more complicated than it needs to be. Decision-making is tough, don't get me wrong. And bad decisions have consequences. But if we're following Psalm 25, seeking to be the person God wants us to be and obeying him in all the ways we know how, we can make a decision and trust that God is guiding us, just as he said he would. His guidance likely won't come through lights in the sky or a flock of doves in your driveway, and I wouldn't consult any fortune cookies. But as you prayerfully read his word, prayerfully obey his commands, prayerfully consult his church, and prayerfully listen for any promptings of his Spirit, you can be confident that your Good Shepherd will guide you in the way he wants you to go.

That's a promise you can claim in prayer.

THE SHEEP PRAYER

For the last several years I've found comfort in a "sheep prayer" that I pray during big decisions. It's a prayer directed by a "good news/bad news" truth.

The bad news first: when God chose an animal to stand for his people in the Bible, he chose a sheep. Not a strong lion, or a wise owl, or a diligent ant. Not even his "favorite animal," the dove. No, he picked a sheep.

Sheep are idiots. They can't run fast, they have bad eyesight, and they can't defend themselves. They sometimes step into streams and drown, or walk right off of cliffs. If they stumble, they often end up "cast," which is the technical term for being stuck upside-down. (Like turtles, if they end up on their back, they can't flip themselves back over.) Sheep are basically walking feed-bags. And that's what God calls us. Bad news: even the wisest, most successful, and most insightful of us are sheep. That means we're in trouble. But it sets us up for the good news.

The good news: we have a shepherd who promises to guard, straighten, and correct our paths if we trust in him. If sheep get to where sheep need to go, it's never because of their competence as sheep. It's because their shepherd is competent to guide them. We have an omni-competent shepherd.

And we need one. God gave up on our decision-making ability back in the Garden of Eden. From Genesis 3 onwards, it has always been clear that if God's people were going to make it through life, it wouldn't be because of our erudite decision-making capacity or skillful warrior instincts. It would be because God led us.

Proverbs 3:5-6 says it plainly: "Trust in the LORD with all your heart, and do not lean on your own understanding. In all your ways acknowledge him, and he will make straight your paths."

That verse has two parts: yours and God's.

Your part? "Trust in the LORD with all your heart" and "acknowledge him" in all your ways—that is, obey everything you know he's told you to do.

His part? "He will make straight your paths." The New King James Version puts that line like this: "He shall direct your paths."

We can read that verse as if it were a contract—if you do your part, God will do his. My pastor when I was growing up made me draw a little wall between the two clauses to remind myself of what was my responsibility and what was God's. I get the "in all your ways acknowledge him" side of the wall. He lives on the "make straight your paths" side.

Most of our stress comes from worrying about what's on God's side of the wall! "What if I make a wrong decision?" "What if this sends me in a 'crooked' direction?"

God says, *Get back on your side of the wall.*

But what if, after acknowledging him in everything I know how to, there is some crucial piece of information I am still missing? How was I supposed to know the choice that landed me on page 47 would put me into the mouth of a volcano?

That's his side of the wall. And that's where trusting in the Lord comes in. He even tells you not to lean on "your own understanding"! In other words, don't even depend on your ability to discern his will! Depend on God's willingness to guide you. Bad news: your limited understanding will never be sufficient. Good news: your omnicompetent shepherd's infinite understanding will always be. He knows what's on page 47 and on page 847. He knows every page of the whole book (Psalm 139:16). You can trust him.

Here's how the "sheep prayer," therefore, comes out for me:

> *"Lord, I have this decision to make, and I have done my best to listen to you and figure it out in every possible way, and I've taken good counsel and I've prayed about it, and now, God, this is what I think I am going to do.*

But God, I know I am a sheep, and sheep are idiots, so I have no confidence in my ability to make this decision. But I do have confidence in your competence and compassion as my Good Shepherd to guide me. So, if this is not the right decision, I'm asking you to take your rod and your staff and to stop me going that way, and to get me to where I do need to go."

This is a humbling thing to pray but an empowering way to live. We don't need to lean on ourselves and figure it out for ourselves, and then spend life worrying that we may have got it wrong. We lean on him, follow him, and spend life knowing that he has us right where he wants us to be. Even our own mistakes, and even other people's wrongdoing, cannot prevent him guiding us in paths of righteousness (Psalm 23:3). If you entrust yourself to him, he won't let you mess it up, nor will he let others mess it up. No one messes with our Shepherd's sheep! He laid down his life for them. At this point, he has more invested in your life than you do—he spilled his own blood to save you. He won't let anybody destroy his treasured possession (Isaiah 43:3-5).

All of which sets us up for David's final piece of counsel from Psalm 25.

DEPENDENT ON HIS GRACE

Fourth, and finally, the person whom God guides is the person who depends on his grace. It is not always easy to trust God. But it is always right to—because he promises his grace to those who trust him, a grace that knows no limits.

Throughout Psalm 25 David talks about God's deliverance, and the pinnacle of this deliverance is expressed in the psalm's central verse: "All the paths of the LORD are steadfast love and faithfulness" (Psalm 25:10).

The word translated "steadfast love" is *hesed*: God's unconditional, wholly committed covenant love for his people. If you are trusting Christ, then everything God is doing in your life now is based on unconditional love. God is not holding grudges against you for past sins, even the most perverse ones. Nor is he disappointed with you for present and persistent flaws. He's most definitely not ashamed of you because of something someone else has done to you.

If you think God is simply "putting up" with you—or if you think he is, candidly, a little annoyed with you—then you'll struggle to believe that he wants blessing for you. Anytime you experience God's abundant goodness to you, you'll be waiting for the other shoe to drop. You'll be worrying that God is up there thinking, *You don't think you really deserve this good thing, do you? I'm going to have to make something bad happen to you to even the score.* Every blessing in your life will be met with fear, as you assume that a just God can't let you to be too happy for too long.

But that's the opposite of how the gospel teaches us to think. The good news of the gospel is that what God gives you, and where God guides you, is never based on your worthiness or performance. It's based on what he's given you in Jesus. Thank God! Because of the finished work of Christ, he sees you now only as a beloved, innocent child over whom he dotes (Zephaniah 3:17).

In other words, the other shoe already dropped—on Jesus. He took your sin and the condemnation it deserved, so that "there is therefore no condemnation for those who are in Christ Jesus" (Romans 8:1).

Nothing remains for us but joy and happiness: "the blessing of the LORD makes rich, and he adds no sorrow with it" (Proverbs 10:22).

When we depend on his grace, we can rest securely knowing that God guides us only in paths of blessing. Surely goodness and mercy will follow us for every second of every day for the rest of eternity, and we will dwell in his house as beloved children forever—the happy sheep of his pasture. All the promises of God are yes in Christ Jesus!

SO, BEFORE YOU PRAY...

This last chapter has been far less about praying for guidance than about becoming the kind of person whom God guides. That's deliberate.

It is good to pray. It is right to ask him to help us, change us, and lead us. But it is also necessary to ask how we see God and whether we understand how he sees us in Christ, if we have received him.

Effective praying comes from the favored status that God has given us in Christ. Prayer that moves heaven comes from a heart that is confident in Jesus. Prayer that brings the peace that passes all understanding is prayer that arises from the understanding that God is in all things molding his children into the likeness of their big Brother and from the assurance that he will not fail or falter in his purpose.

So, before you pray for guidance, ask yourself how you see God and how you think he sees you. Ask whether you've assumed your position as his beloved child, a sheep he has sworn to protect. Have you received his offer of forgiveness and eternal life? If not, you can do so right now. Then ask whether you are someone committed to knowing his ways, obeying his decrees, trusting his promises, and depending on his grace.

Then, you can pray to him with confidence: "Our Father…"

CONCLUSION

I want to finish by giving a few really practical suggestions that will help you start a daily prayer time if you've never really had one, or revitalize it if it's fallen into a rut. The distance between good intention and change is spanned by a plan of action, and there's no point in reading a book like this about prayer if it doesn't lead to you actually praying.

So here are ten suggestions. Yes, I said ten, but this is kind of a grab-bag of ideas. You don't have to do all of them! Use whatever helps.

1. *Riff off of the Lord's Model Prayer.* To be clear, I'm no musician. But of all the ways to use the "Model Prayer," this one made the most sense to me. Take each line of Jesus' model as your melody line, let it saturate your heart, and then riff off of it. Look to the Spirit to help and guide you as you do it. For the last few years, I've opened my daily prayer time by doing this for at least five minutes, and it's helped me greatly.

2. *Use the acrostic ACTS to help you pray.* This framework is actually very similar to the prayer Jesus gave, though with slightly different handles.

A – Adoration. Spend time thinking about the character of God and praising him for who he is. (This is different than thanksgiving. That's gratitude for what he has done—this is worship for who he is.)

C – Confession. Spend time confessing specific ways you've sinned. It may help to have a few well-known confessions written out to use as a jumping-off point.

T – Thanksgiving. Give thanks to God for the cross, on which he nailed all those sins you just confessed and took them from you so that you can be forgiven. Then express your gratitude for his daily blessings to you as well. Be specific. Thank him for little things as well as big ones.

S – Supplication. Honestly, this is just a fancy word for "asking." I guess they didn't just use "Ask" because ACTA is not as catchy as ACTS.

3. *Use a prayer companion.* I love *The Valley of Vision*, a collection of Puritan prayers; *The Songs of Jesus* by Tim and Kathy Keller, which prays through the Psalms; and the *Five Things to Pray* series, which takes a passage of Scripture and gives five areas to pray from it. I use these at various points to jump-start my prayers.

4. *Set aside two or three brief times a day for prayer rather than one long one.* What torpedoes us after reading a book on prayer is that we resolve, "Ok! No more messing around. I will rise early and pray for two hours, every day, without fail." And you manage it for a week, maybe two—though likely you falter on the very first morning. Instead, why not aim to pray for five minutes in the morning when you wake up, for five minutes right after lunch, and for five minutes just before you go to bed (or at whatever times work for you)? Start with these, and as you start to enjoy those times with your Father, you'll find yourself praying longer.

5. *Take a morning walk and pray out loud.* Seriously. Don't feel weird. Jesus prayed out loud. The first Christians prayed out loud. Praying out loud helps us focus on what we're saying and keeps us concentrating on actually praying. (If you have never started praying in your head, only to realize a few minutes later that you're thinking about this morning's meeting or today's to-do list, or what's going to happen next in that Netflix series you're enjoying, then you're a very rare and special Christian with iron-strength focus. For the rest of us, we need help with concentrating.) Plus, learning to pray out loud prepares us to pray out loud with others, which is a way to encourage others. Nothing builds my faith like hearing someone else express theirs in prayer. If you don't want to be overheard by others in your home as you pray out loud, take a walk. Talk to your Father. Out loud.

6. *Set reminders on your calendar to pray for specific needs at specific times.* Have an alarm that goes off at the same time each day to remind you to pray for someone or some situation. Prayer apps like EchoPrayer or PrayerMate can help you organize and keep track of the things you want to pray about. I use one of these apps, with "cards" for different people in my life and different situations. On each card I have specific things to pray for those people or situations, coupled with Scripture verses that correspond to my request.

7. *Pray in the moment with people.* If another believer shares a concern or problem with you, don't just promise to pray for them (though that's great, obviously). Actually pray for them, right then and there. Here's your line: "Thank you so much for sharing that. Actually, could I take a moment now to pray for you?"

8. Prayer-walk your neighborhood, office, or school. Don't do it in a creepy way—no one wants to see you walking round your office with your hands raised, anointing the cubicle dividers with oil or looking like you're calling down fire on your neighbor's house. Walk about naturally, praying silently for people and for places, and for anything else that the Spirit prompts you to lift up to God. Seeing people and knowing about their needs invigorates my times of intercession.

9. If you have kids, let them hear you pray. (Again, this means praying out loud.) Let them hear you apply faith to your situation, wrestle with God's promises, and pour out your heart to him. Nothing disciples someone quite so well as letting them hear you pray. My dad says of the hundreds of sermons he heard his first pastor preach that, he can scarcely remember any of them. But he remembers how his pastor prayed for him, and with him for others. Ask your kids to pray too. You could use the kids' version of ACTS—WITH: Wow, I'm sorry, Thanks, Help.

10. Enjoy your time with your Father. Remember the story I told you about my dad? God is excited to meet with you. "Pray" is not a religious task to accomplish; it's an invitation to lay your burdens down at Jesus' feet, to share your heart with him, and to be with the one in whose presence is the fullness of joy and at whose right hand are pleasures forevermore (Psalm 16:11). It really is our greatest privilege. "See what kind of love the Father has given to us, that we should be called children of God" (1 John 3:1).

> *What a friend we have in Jesus,*
> *All our griefs with him to share,*

> *What a privilege to carry,*
> *Everything to God in prayer!*

Above all, though, just start. Prayer is a muscle that grows as you use it. The more you pray, the more you'll know how to pray, the more you'll desire to pray, and the more you'll start to see answers to your prayers.

I read somewhere that if you do something for 21 days, it becomes a habit that is harder to break than to keep. So I challenge you, on finishing this book, to pray for five minutes, three times a day, for 21 days—and see where the Spirit takes it from there.

Don't let regular, passionate, hope-filled prayer stay in the realm of "Things I ought to do." Start, and let it move to the list of "Things I love to do."

Just start.

Your Father is waiting.

Just ask.

BIBLIOGRAPHY

Mark Batterson, *The Circle Maker* (Zondervan, 2011)

Arthur Bennett, *The Valley of Vision* (Banner of Truth, 1975)

Vance Christie, *Timeless Stories: God's Incredible Work in the Lives of Inspiring Christians* (Christian Focus, 2010)

Kevin DeYoung, *Just Do Something* (Moody, 2009)

Elyse Fitzpatrick and Jessica Thompson, *Give them Grace* (Crossway, 2011)

J.D. Greear, *Jesus Continued...* (Zondervan, 2014)

A.A. Hodge, *Evangelical Theology* (Banner of Truth, 1990)

Timothy Keller, *Judges For You* (The Good Book Company, 2013)

Timothy Keller, *Prayer* (Viking, 2014)

Timothy Keller, *The Songs of Jesus* (Viking, 2015: published in the UK by Hodder Faith as *My Rock My Refuge*)

Carl Laferton, ed. *Five Things to Pray* series (The Good Book Company)

C.S. Lewis, *A Grief Observed* (HarperCollins, 2001)

Paul Miller, *A Praying Life* (NavPress, 2009)

John Newton, *Select Letters of John Newton* (Banner of Truth, 2011)

J.I. Packer, *Knowing God* (3rd edition: Hodder & Stoughton Religious/Hodder Faith, 2005)

Eugene Peterson, *Answering God* (HarperOne, 1991)

Milton Vincent, *A Gospel Primer for Christians* (Focus Publishing, 2008)

ACKNOWLEDGMENTS

Every book I have written has been written first and foremost for members of The Summit Church, in Raleigh-Durham, NC, whom I have been privileged to pastor now for 20 years. I love them. They are such a generous and responsive people. If there's one thing God is pressing in on our church right now, it is to pray. Prayer is not the preparation for the ministry of the church; it *is* the ministry of the church.

It is impossible to overstate my gratitude to Chris Gaynor, our pastor of prayer and worship. Chris, our longest-tenured staff member, has done more to cultivate a spirit of prayer at our church than anyone else. He championed it when no one else did. God speaks to me through his prayers. He has that wonderful gift of faith, whereby God plants in our hearts the vision of what he wants to do before he does it, inviting us to trust him for it. The fruitfulness The Summit Church has experienced has been, in large part, owing to Chris's prayers. As he loves to repeat from Andrew Murray, "The one who mobilizes the church to pray will do more for the Great Commission than any other." Thank you, Chris.

It is also impossible to overstate what I owe to my dad. I dedicated this book to my mom, but my dad is probably the subject of the majority of the illustrations in this book. As a young boy, I knew exactly where to find him each morning between 4:30 and 5:30 a.m.: on his knees, with his Bible, talking to God. Growing up, I never doubted God's existence because I saw him working in my dad's life.

Throughout this project, Carl Laferton and the crew at The Good Book Company were (ahem) an answer to prayer (see what I did there?). Carl edits with the rare combination of wit, wisdom, and humility. In achieving the final product that you hold here, I am highly indebted to him (even if he tries to deflect the praise). I doubt this paragraph will make it through editing.

Chris Pappalardo, The Summit's editor, has been helping me craft the ideas in these pages long before they were fit for print. I can't imagine writing sermons without him at my right hand, helping me sound like the most faithful version of myself. The message I proclaim is clearer and more compelling because of his erudite skill and indomitable dedication.

Dana Leach runs J.D. Greear Ministries, tackling the thousand organizational challenges that would otherwise take me down. She keeps going after everyone else quits, and believes when the rest of us falter. Without her, books like this simply wouldn't exist.

If Dana runs J.D. Greear Ministries, Aly Rand runs, well, J.D. Greear. I sometimes play an anxious game called, "What Person Would Make Me Panic If They Left?" Aly tops the list. Just typing that sentence made me nervous, and I'm going to stop now to pray and offer vows to God to keep her here forever. I simply cannot imagine replacing all that she does with any other single individual.

For the last couple of years, Daniel Riggs has done whatever odd jobs I've asked of him, and he's done them with humility and reliability. One day Daniel will be a great pastor. He's already a great leader. Selfishly, I hope it's a while from now.

Lastly, I would be remiss if I passed over my wife, Veronica, who consistently gives me the greatest gift an author can receive—a reminder that real life matters most. No one thinks more of my ministry, but at the same time no one is less impressed that I write books. And she really believes in prayer. Perhaps the greatest blessing in the process of writing this book has been learning to pour out our hearts to God together daily. And my four kids—Kharis, Allie, Ryan, and Adon—are awesome. They love the ideas in these books and have cheered me on in writing them. Right now, they are the subject of a lot of my prayers. I am confident that soon they will be the evidence that prayer works. Love you guys.

BIBLICAL | RELEVANT | ACCESSIBLE

At The Good Book Company, we are dedicated to helping Christians and local churches grow. We believe that God's growth process always starts with hearing clearly what he has said to us through his timeless word—the Bible.

Ever since we opened our doors in 1991, we have been striving to produce Bible-based resources that bring glory to God. We have grown to become an international provider of user-friendly resources to the Christian community, with believers of all backgrounds and denominations using our books, Bible studies, devotionals, evangelistic resources, and DVD-based courses.

We want to equip ordinary Christians to live for Christ day by day, and churches to grow in their knowledge of God, their love for one another, and the effectiveness of their outreach.

Call us for a discussion of your needs or visit one of our local websites for more information on the resources and services we provide.

Your friends at The Good Book Company

thegoodbook.com | thegoodbook.co.uk
thegoodbook.com.au | thegoodbook.co.nz
thegoodbook.co.in